Withdrawn

HOW NOT TO BE AN ANTIQUES DEALER

HOW NOT TO BE AN ANTIQUES DEALER

EVERYTHING I'VE LEARNT, THAT NOBODY TOLD ME

Drew Pritchard

EBURY SPOTLIGHT

Ebury Spotlight, an imprint of Ebury Publishing
20 Vauxhall Bridge Road
London SW1V 2SA

Ebury Spotlight is part of the Penguin Random House group of companies whose addresses can be found at global.penguinrandomhouse.com

Copyright © Drew Pritchard 2023

Drew Pritchard has asserted his right to be identified as the author of this Work in accordance with the Copyright, Designs and Patents Act 1988

First published by Ebury Spotlight in 2023

www.penguin.co.uk

A CIP catalogue record for this book is available from the British Library

ISBN 9781529149609

Typeset in 11.5/18.6pt Sabon GEO MT Std
by Jouve (UK), Milton Keynes
Printed and bound in Great Britain by Clays Ltd, Elcograf S.p.A.

The authorised representative in the EEA is Penguin Random House Ireland, Morrison Chambers, 32 Nassau Street, Dublin D02 YH68

Penguin Random House is committed to a sustainable future for our business, our readers and our planet. This book is made from Forest Stewardship Council® certified paper.

For Gwen
Love Rhys

CONTENTS

INTRODUCTION   1

What Exactly Is This Business?   6

1. GETTING SET UP   13

Things You're Going to Need   16
Do Your Research   25
Restoration   35

2. BUYING   43

How to Buy   45
   Discretion   47
   The Magic and Buying
   What You Love   56
Where to Buy   61
   Buying Dealer to Dealer   62
     Stand On   70
   Buying Privately   75
     The Three Ds   86

Buying at Fairs	87
Matching Pairs	93
Go Against the Flow	98
Buying at Auction	99

3. SELLING   119

Preparing Your Stock for Sale	121
Set Your Price	124
Move Your Stock Quickly	131
Trade to Trade	137
Appro	144
Running Your Own Shop	147
It's a 24-7 Business	161
Selling Online	162
Packing and Shipping	166
Restocking	172
Taking a Loss and Cashflow	175

4. DOING IT THE RIGHT WAY   181

Negotiation	183
You Are What You Sell	186
Keeping the Odd Bit	191
Things You Shouldn't Say or Do	197
Keep Going	205

ACKNOWLEDGEMENTS   215

INTRODUCTION

Ever since I can remember, I wanted to be an antiques dealer.

This life has given me everything, and not just monetarily. That helps of course, but what I really mean is the opportunities and experiences it's provided for me. For instance, sitting on a hill in Italy with the sun on my face, jeans filthy from crawling around some attic, surrounded by things I've just bought, things I love and understand. It's the friends I've made, the knowledge acquired. It's rescuing a long-lost item, not for the glory or the money, but for the sheer unadulterated joy of sharing it with other people.

It's the pleasure I get from reading. The fact that a bit of information left on a page by someone from way back when can open up a whole new world amazes me. The moment it dawns on you that all styles, all genres from all ages, are linked, that you don't get one without the other, the world becomes a bigger place. Understanding this, and therefore better understanding yourself and your work, is what makes you go up another level. And it doesn't stop. There is always something more to learn, and your knowledge and insight will always be enhanced by what you read.

It's an appreciation of the things we find, things made by people – call it art, or call it craftsmanship. It's what these things say to us that's so important. If you can convey the same sense of excitement you felt when you first found a piece, pass it on to someone else by the way it's positioned in a showroom, the way it's photographed or the way it's described in a listing, and sell the item that's so inspired you, that's the key to opening the world. But like all wonders, they're hard won, and the journey might sometimes feel like purgatory. That's just the way it is. But the way a table adorned with a lamp and a photograph can affect a room, a mood and possibly a life, is inspirational. It's magic, the reason we do what we do. I don't really understand it, or even want to – I just love being a part of it, creating something and seeing the magic happen.

This is an entire life if you want it. It feels like a gift, and I cherish every single moment. It's not something you throw away when you're finished. It's

INTRODUCTION

not an enchantment or fad. And it's so much more than just dead people's stuff. It's rich and layered. It's artistic and keeps you grounded. It's joyful and cold-hearted. It's jealous and bewitching in equal measure. Above all else it's enriching: you will learn something new every day, good or bad, and you'll gain something from every situation you encounter. It has changed everything for me and continues to do so yearly, daily, hourly – it's all I've ever wanted to do.

When it comes down to it, it's all about taste. I can't teach you that – you're born with it or you're not. The 'eye' cannot be taught. Sorry, but that's the truth. The rest can, and, in some small part, that's what I hope we can achieve here. Just now I said there is no manual to teach you how to be an antiques dealer, but I hope this book will help you if you want to get started in this business. With that said, I want to make something clear: what you're about to read is just the basics, and it's not some hard and fast set of dos and don'ts; it's not me telling you this is the only way to do something – it's just my opinion. I don't have all the answers. But I have done a lot, and I've been around. I've tried it all, so I suppose it does give me some perspective to pass on.

Dealing in antiques has given me a life that continues to be unbelievably good fun. It's broken down imaginary barriers and created rather than broken dreams. I never want it to stop. I hope it will mean the same to you, so let's get to it, shall we?

What Exactly Is This Business?

Before we begin, before you take the plunge and leave your job or invest some money in stock, you need to fully understand what you're getting yourself into. The antiques business is tough and it takes a lifetime. For that reason it's not for the faint-hearted. Being mad keen is brilliant – enthusiasm is half the battle – but you also need to know what you're doing.

If you're just getting started, you probably don't know very much yet – don't pretend you do. People do this all the time. You'll immediately get dealers' backs up and you won't learn anything. You've got to be honest with yourself and with others. It's fine not to know very much at the beginning, because I'm going to share with you as much as I can and answer the tons of questions you might have.

It's also OK to be nervous. That's exactly how it should be – nervous is good because you're going to work seven days a week every week and travel thousands and thousands of miles. You're going to meet incredibly interesting people and you're going to meet some people who are not going to be as helpful or as friendly as they could be. You're going to have wonderful times, but you're going to have tough times too. The first ten or so years will be the hardest. Make it beyond those ten and you'll be well on your way to achieving what you want in this business. After that, there are no limits. You can go as far as you want. You can decide where you want to be and stay at that level or you can decide to go up, down or sideways.

But because there are no limits, you can get lost in this 'magical' world of antiques. You therefore need to figure out what you want. By that I mean you need to really think about which area of the business you want to work in. You might not end up there – it's not mandatory. Despite what you aim for and where you start out, you might end up somewhere totally different.

There are lots of different parts of the antiques business – from restorers to porters, to shippers, to photographers, to valuers, to dealers, to gallerists. I started as a restorer and then became an architectural antiques dealer, and I've ended up as a fine English furniture dealer and interior decorator supplier, with lots of other things in between. As you learn more and are exposed to new areas of the antiques world, you'll find other things that fascinate you that you didn't know were out there when you began. It's all part of the learning curve. It's like a stepladder effect. You start at the bottom rung, which could be fireplaces, and then that leads you on to overmantel mirrors, which leads you on to lighting, which leads you on to rugs. It's a progression, with one step leading up to the next, and you stop wherever you feel most comfortable. But there's no way of knowing where that will be at the outset. So, just start on the thing that you love, and learn as much as you can about it. That knowledge, whether it relates to design, manufacture, scale or history, might then lead you on to other things, because everything is interlocking in the antiques business.

In my experience, once you're in, you're in for life. I always call the antiques trade 'Hotel California' – you could check out if you wanted to, but most people never leave. I don't know anybody who's got into the business who has left, apart from perhaps a couple of guys who made a big noise when they first arrived then disappeared off the face of the earth, never to be heard from again. It's a hell of a life – and what a life – but you have to be in it for the long haul. Just because you've watched *Antiques*

INTRODUCTION

Roadshow for 20 years and made 50 quid selling something to your mate in the pub does not make you an antiques dealer. It's a long, long road if you want to get to the point where you can really call yourself a dealer.

The reality is 5am starts when you're still covered in muck from loading the night before. The reality is packing the van so nothing is forgotten and nothing gets broken. The reality is booking tickets for your stand at the antiques fair. It's standing in the rain for three days on end or sleeping in the back of the van. It's not being able to shower or even wash your hands. It's having no money whatsoever. It's getting ripped off or robbed. I remember one Newark fair when I had to employ a bodyguard to make sure I didn't get mugged and nobody picked the cash from my pockets that I'd worked my arse off to get in the first place.

It's also hooning down the M6 in crappy weather hoping you're going to sell something and make enough money to get back up the road – it really hits home when you have no choice but to make a sale. That's where I've been countless times, and it's brutal. In the early days, the big question was always whether the van was going to make it. There was no guarantee because it was as ropey as hell, but it was all I could afford. I'd be worrying all the way to Newark from North Wales, fearing a breakdown.

There is so much people don't realise, layer upon layer that you don't know about until you're in the middle of it. To be an antiques dealer is to be an artist, designer and curator. You're a photographer, a buyer, a van driver and a salesman all at the same time, and you have to be able to jump from dealing with a demolition contractor at 8.30 in the morning to lunch with a lord at 1pm before hitting the pub with a load of other dealers and not getting away before midnight. It's deals all the way, and the most natural dealers are at it when they're 11 or 12 years old. That's how it was with me. At that age I didn't know what I do now, but it just made sense, and I've been doing nothing else since.

And it has been great fun, as you'll see when I tell you about some of the experiences I've had down the years that probably shouldn't be repeated. But right now, I want to make sure you know what you're letting yourself in for. Having to make money out of it rather than just dabbling scares the hell out of some people, particularly if they've come from another job where they've been earning a decent salary. I've only ever had one job, and I never got paid very much, so for me it didn't matter. But some

INTRODUCTION

people give up careers to start this one, and that can be pretty scary.

The reality of this business is continuity. If you don't sell what you've bought, you won't have any money to carry on trading. It's like Monopoly. If you run out of money you're out of the game and that can happen very easily. You have to constantly turn money over in order to keep going. But if you've done it right, if you've bought well and the van made it, and you're at the fair all set up and ready to go and you sell your first few things, a weight is lifted. The excitement kicks in – that phenomenal rush of adrenalin. That's the moment when a dealer is made – it really is that difficult yet simple at the same time.

For the people who are good at it there's an overpowering want, a need, an all-consuming hunger to get into the business and do well. All they think about is antiques and dealing, because there is so much satisfaction and wonder to be had from a world where every item you come across has its own story and can potentially make you money.

What I want to do with this book is give you as much help as I can, but it's not the beginning or the end – it's just a guide, remember? Something to refer to so you won't be totally lost when you first start. It took me years to learn the basics, because when I started there was no internet and no social media where you could pick the brains of those who'd been there and done it. So think of this as a map to help navigate the initial hurdles. Once you've overcome them, the rest is what you make of it.

1
GETTING SET UP

The most important thing you can acquire in this business is knowledge. Knowledge comes from experience and the only way to broaden your experience is to submerge yourself in the world of antiques. I spoke to a bloke at a fair the other day who told me he'd taken a part-time job in an antiques shop to try and get a little experience before he branched out on his own. That's exactly the sort of thing I would advise anyone new to the business to do. Being around things, touching them, looking at them, walking away then coming back to look again, you can't do enough of that, especially in the early days – it's vital. Once you've done that and the ambition to go further has been cemented, you have to figure out what to do. Moving from a 'dabble' to a serious business where you have to make money is a very hard thing to do.

Things You're Going to Need

No. 1 – Money

You can't start out in this business without some cash and the more you can save up for the initial investment the better. I started with £200, but that was decades ago, so if we bring that forward you probably need about £2,000 these days. Ideally, I'd recommend £5,000. The more you have the better, of course, as the amount of money you start with is some indicator of how much you're going to earn. It's simple economics: the more you start with, the more you're able to make, or that's how it should be, although it doesn't always work out like that. Mistakes are made; none of us get it right all the time. Remember this is not like any other business. Everything is what you make it.

I am an appalling businessman. I now know how to make a quid, of course, but I had to work very hard to find the first £200. When I was starting out, an old dealer told me something I've never forgotten: 'The hardest money you will make is the first quid.'

Money is your tool. If you've got £200 and you can buy something, you're likely to make a percentage of £200. So, £20 or £40. If you've got £2,000, your percentage is going to be £200 or £400. If you've got £10,000, you're going to make £1,000 or £2,000 or even £4,000. The more you put in, the more you're going to make. It's the same regardless of what you're buying or selling. If you start with more money, you're able to buy more stock, and you're able to buy better stock.

It can also be useful to buy a wider range of smaller items to mitigate your risk a little bit when you're first starting out, although it does depend on what level of knowledge you have. But if you're not really sure about the things you're seeing, try and buy a range of pieces that you like and that are in your wheelhouse, whether that's china, or Second World War American flying jackets, or fine paintings, or watches, or whatever. Buy a selection that gives people a little bit of choice. It's like spread betting – I'll make 10 per cent on this and 20 per cent on that; I might make 5 per cent on that; I might not get rid of this but I can swap it.

If you are confident and you think you can buy one good thing and you think you can get rid of it – you know enough about it and you have a market for it – going in slightly deeper and buying a better piece at the beginning can be very profitable. But you are setting yourself up for a fall if it goes wrong, because you've put all your eggs in one basket. So, it's not ideal when you're a beginner.

It's also worth saying here that whatever start-up cash you manage to get together is not just for stock – you need to be able to cover your overheads too. The antiques business is a juggling act between spending your money, gambling on items and maintaining enough working capital to keep going. I can be reckless and emotional when it comes to business, but I try and keep some money back in case I stumble on that 'once in a lifetime' item. I'd also recommend a backstop of three months' worth of rent, mortgage, bills, etc. It's incredibly hard to do because the temptation is to buy, buy, buy, and you need to do that to keep turning stock over. But you also need to be able to pay your mortgage, your diesel, your electricity and be able to buy yourself a sarnie or two.

You do fly by the seat of your pants sometimes – that's just the nature of the business. Every day is different. You never know what you're going to come across. My accountant used to look at my books and tell me as a business model it made no sense whatsoever. At the time I was carrying a fairly large stock of architectural salvage (see page 57), with an £80,000 overdraft, and I was still on the road every day spending money. You have to find your own level and go with what you're comfortable with – there is no hard and fast rule when it comes to backstop and buying. My advice would be to make sure you have enough for the basics and buy to sell as quickly as possible. At the outset, the maximum you're going to have at any one time is probably a van load, so turn that over, make the margin and the business will start to take shape. Then you can assess where you are, what you need to do next, how much you're comfortable spending and how much you need in reserve.

No. 2 – Transport

You're going to need transport because you're going to do a lot of travelling. You could sit in front of a computer all day and do it that way, but I don't recommend it. If you do that, you won't see the best things, you won't buy the best things and you won't meet anybody. So, you need a reliable, comfortable, cheap to run, tough-as-old-boots car and/or van. The right vehicle will make you money, because the antiques business is all about logistics. You need to be mobile. If a customer wants to see an item, you can take it to show them. If you go to see something and want to buy it, you can take it away with you there and then, saving on shipping costs. It's on-the-ground dealing, talking to customers, talking to buyers, talking to sellers, where the money's made.

This is important: you need a van or estate car if you're dealing with anything big. If it's stamps you're into, you can go out on a moped, but it needs to be reliable. Other than that, you need four good wheels, which is why most dealers end up driving Volvo or Mercedes estates. Back when I began there was a big thing between Volvo and Mercedes estates. The posher dealers had the Mercedes, the others had the Volvos. They're both good, as they can both cope with the mileage. I've been through a dozen or more Mercedes estates and a couple of Volvos. Before I got to the estates I had a Volkswagen Beetle with a roof rack, then I moved on to an Astra van that came out of a scrapyard. After that it was a Mercedes 208 that came from next door to a scrapyard and then I started making a few quid and got a Mercedes estate and a Mercedes Sprinter van, which kept me going for eight years.

Whatever kind of vehicle you choose is up to you, but I'd recommend you get an automatic – make it dead comfortable, because you're going to be living in it. Buy the best you possibly can that'll do what you need it to do. It's probably going to be your only

GETTING SET UP

vehicle, so it needs to be good – you're a long way from buying Porsches. And your van/car is a tool, so look after it, and keep it serviced and clean. Don't think it's cool to drive around in a ratty old thing with dents in the side and crap all over the dashboard.

Finally, don't advertise your business on the side of your car or van. If you've watched my TV show, you'll have noticed that my van doesn't have a sign. It's blank for a very good reason. If it were marked Drew Pritchard Antiques, it would get broken into.

No. 3 – A mobile phone

This might sound obvious, but you don't just need a decent mobile phone – you need to know how to use it properly. I get so many people saying to me, 'Oh, I don't do email.' 'Oh, I don't know how to send a text.' 'Oh, I don't know how to use WhatsApp or take a picture.' If that's you, I'm afraid you're going to have to learn. Mobile phones have been commonplace for around 30 years now. I got my first one when I was 23, and it opened up the world to me. So, learn how to take a good photograph with your phone and how to send it correctly. In fact, learn how to send multiple photographs. Learn how to send voice notes. Learn how to drop pins. Learn how to use your satnav correctly. This is stuff you're going to use every single day as an antiques dealer. You will live on the road and your phone can make you money.

Often, someone will contact me and say they have something I might be interested in. It happened recently when a guy I knew got in touch and said he had a piece of furniture I might like. It was £1,000. I went to see it and said, 'I'll have that.' I then photographed it with my phone and sent the photo to a customer with a price that included my profit. The customer said, 'All right, fine, I'll have it. My shipper will come and get it.' I never picked up the piece I'd bought or put it in the back of my car and moved it, but I'd made money on it by sending a picture.

A good phone is maybe the most important tool you've got at your disposal. At the moment, I've got one of the latest iPhones with the best cameras. It's an incredible tool, and I'm probably only taking advantage of 1 per cent of its potential, but that's all I need. I can update my Instagram, Facebook and Twitter accounts on it. I can upload items to my website on it, and I can take stuff off it. I can send photographs, receive calls, email – all of that. It's obvious but lots of people in the business don't use their phones enough.

GETTING SET UP

No. 4 – The right forms of payment

That means a bank and/or credit card, a cheque book (although less and less these days) and online payment ability on your phone. Cash isn't actually that important. Most people don't want it. Unless you're doing a fair or flea market it's rarely used now – it's not like the old days.

No. 5 – Comfortable shoes

I know this one might sound a bit ridiculous, but you're going to be doing an awful lot of walking. You drive somewhere and park your car, then you're on foot, maybe for hours on end. You might be at an auction house walking round looking at each lot or you might be at a fair. On the way back you might call in on two or three dealers, pop into a museum or visit a restorer, then it's back to your car, all of it walking, and for that you need comfortable shoes.

No. 6 – Computer skills

These days you have to be able to work online or you're going nowhere. Like with your phone – which is really a computer in your pocket – knowing how to use a computer and be online is a must, even if it's just so you can contact your international clients. I had someone in North Carolina contact me at about half past ten one night, asking for an extra picture of a pair of bookcases that I had for sale. I went on to my home computer and sent them a picture from my database, and they woke up the following morning and bought them. So, sending that late-night email made me money. We'll come back to working online later, but at the outset you've got to learn the basics, even if you are a technophobe.

No. 7 – A very understanding husband, wife, partner or family

You'll need (and this is really important) your loved ones to be very understanding. If they're not interested in what you're doing, if they don't want to know, it will make things more difficult for you, because if you have the kind of passion you need to succeed, then you'll require support, not someone who's going to get in the way.

No. 8 – Storage

Depending on what area of the business you're going to specialise in, your storage facility can be anything from a shed or garage to some sort of lock-up, so long as it's dry and secure. Ideally, you don't want money tied up in a premises when you're starting out, so use that shed in your garden or even your living room. When I began, I used my entire tiny rented house in Chapel Street, Conwy. It was full of stock, as were my van outside, my parents' garage, and, yes, my gran's shed.

No. 9 – Contacts

Every time you meet somebody new, exchange details. Take their business card and make sure you give them yours. Failing that, take a phone number and give them yours, as well as details of your website or email. Make a connection, shake hands properly, look people in the eye. I read somewhere that a real connection is made with someone if you look them in the eye long enough for the colour to register.

Do Your Research

I think it's important to start as you mean to continue. I've laid out some of the practicalities in the last few pages, but there are also less tangible skills that you need right from the outset.

No. 1 – Knowing your subject

Study your subject inside out, whether it be stamps, carpets, door handles, paintings, porcelain, furnishings or architectural antiques. It could be paintings of nineteenth-century dogs if you want – it doesn't matter what it is, but you need to know it inside out. From there, you might branch out into other subjects, but you need to start somewhere, and being an expert in one thing is better than knowing a little bit about a lot of things.

No. 2 – Following other dealers

You need to have a working knowledge of the dealers in your chosen subject around the world who are the very best at what they do. If you are a fireplace dealer, or you're a dealer in garden statuary, or carpets, you need to look at the person at the top of that field. You need to pinpoint who they are and study their businesses, but that doesn't mean copying them. Instead, be inspired. You then need to know who the second-best dealer is and who the third-best dealer is. You need to know who's supplying them and who does their restoration. You need to learn from the best. And the best is a movable field – it's constantly shifting – so you

GETTING SET UP

need to keep on top of it. I know who the best version of me is in America. I know who the best one in France is. I know who the best one in Canada is. I actually know some of them personally. You're all working in the same area, and they are potential suppliers – or customers. If you can make contact with the best in the business and talk to them, you'll learn a huge amount.

No. 3 – Understanding the market

You need to track the auction prices of items in your chosen field that have been sold in the last 20 years. This allows you to have a handle on the market, past and present, which helps when it comes to buying and selling at the right price, and more generally when it comes to spotting trends, and maybe even starting trends if you get to the point where you are influential in the industry. Pricing is essential background information, and one of the best places to get it is auction catalogues (more on which in the next few points), as is keeping an eye on the prices being set by your competitors.

No. 4 – Restoration experts

You need to meet and form relationships with as many of the best restorers as you can. I'll go into restoration in more detail later on, but in terms of research, it's really about identifying the best people and establishing working relationships with people you can trust to do a good job. With some of my restorers over the years, if they've been short of work, I've gone out and bought something for them to fix. I'm not going to make any money as such, but they're making something and I'm keeping them employed.

I'll drive all over the country to meet good restorers. Last year, for example, I drove down to Mid Wales to meet a guy who could do a certain type of welding that I needed done on a piece of furniture. It was a day out of my time, but I wanted to go and meet him. We got on well, and he did the work for me. And now if I need a job done in the future, I have his number and I can call him and we're on first name terms. I know him, and he knows me. We have a working relationship.

No. 5 – Catalogues

You need to buy as many auction catalogues as you can get your hands on. I have a massive collection. I have one in front of me from July 1997. When I'm doing my research, I can have a look and see that the guide price for a Regency mahogany writing table was between £8,000 to £12,000.

GETTING SET UP

I have catalogues going back to 1920, and I buy them from here, there and everywhere. You'll find them in junk shops and in book shops. You'll find them online and at antiques centres and auctions. Buy as many as you can – Bonhams, Christie's, Sotheby's all do them. They can go for anything between £4 and £25 for the good ones. Some of the catalogues are even collectible in their own right. And the best thing is, the person who wrote the catalogue is full of knowledge, and you've got it in front of you, with a picture most of the time. It couldn't be much easier. They are full of invaluable information. Everything you need to know is here.

*

The bottom line is you need to immerse yourself utterly in your chosen field. If you go at it half-arsed, you'll be a half-arsed dealer. You can still make a living, and that's fine – nobody's going to judge you. What I'm saying is, the more you learn, the better you'll be. You need to go to museums and art galleries, look at things and read up on your subject. We're very lucky in the UK that we are surrounded by history, and many of our biggest and best museums and galleries are free. Even if the place doesn't have objects that you're interested in, you can get something out of just looking at the building or how they've displayed their exhibits. Almost everything you'll need to know in this business you can find in a museum – I'm a total museum geek. When I'm filming around the world, I go to museums on my days off. I really do. On my last trip to Germany, I went to Museum Island in Berlin and spent two days there. Just go and look at things and you'll learn so much, as this business is completely visual.

Right now you're probably thinking, *Jesus, that's a lot to do*. You're right. It is. But if you want to be the best you can, that's the job. It's never ending. Trust me, once you start out on this road you need to be committed if you want to really make a go of it and be a success. Instead of sitting there staring blankly at the television every night, pick up a book and read. Grab an auction catalogue. Go through people's websites. Watch an online tutorial by an expert. Watch an online tour of a museum. Instead of a Saturday spent lounging on the sofa watching kicky-ball, get in your car and go to a museum. It can be anything from farm equipment through to a collection of Canalettos. It doesn't matter. You need to learn something and the only way to do that is to immerse yourself in the world of antiques.

GETTING SET UP

It's vast. It's all around you. Pretty much every house in this country has some form of antique. It might be a load of old rubbish. It might be the best thing you've ever seen, an undiscovered treasure – it doesn't matter. It's around us everywhere we go. We're blessed to have buildings, architecture, public art. Being 'fully immersed' in the antiques business is a lifestyle that will keep you employed for the rest of your life, but you can't be lazy. You can't just wait for it all to happen.

Well, I suppose you can be a little lazy. You can know a bit about Barley Twist tables and Ercol furniture and reproduction Chesterfield chairs, and you will make a living, but that's not the way I approach the business. I'm obsessive. I love it and live it. I have the worst formal education you can imagine, and I'm not the only one out there – far from it. I'm forever hearing people say, 'My school was rubbish. My school was this and that.' D'you know what my school did? My school let me down. I didn't learn anything. There were too many kids. In my form alone there were 55 children. In many ways it was a wonderful place, but the teachers spent their energy on the top 10 per cent and the rest just had to hang on in there until we got jobs as van drivers.

I wasn't going to do that. I was determined to make something of myself and use the assets I had. When I left school, I was still an empty vessel. It didn't mean I couldn't learn. You might not have any qualifications, you might have been to a terrible school, you might not be able to write beautifully or converse eloquently on any subject, but it doesn't matter. All these things we're told we should know don't mean anything. I really didn't need to know about oxbow lakes and amoebas, and I still don't. But once I started reading about things that interested me, everything expanded. And that's why I would say to anybody: just start reading something and it will expand your thought processes. And the more you know, the more money you will make.

You can learn at any time in your life. I've been in this business all these years, and I know I'll never stop learning. But you have to start. If you want to make an impression, if you want to get good, you have to put the work in. You can pick up a book at any age. It's never been easier to educate yourself – everything is on the internet. Even now, my favourite thing to do is research. Sitting down and reading is still the absolute best thing you can do. I think it's wonderful.

GETTING SET UP

If you adopt this principle, if you do put those hard yards in, ten years from now you'll have learnt so much you'll be a different person. That's what's so unique about what we do. If you educate yourself, you'll see things differently. You'll be a more interesting person, more rounded. You'll be incredibly knowledgeable and interesting to talk to. You'll be able to walk into a church or an old building and read it. You'll understand the passage of time in architecture, how one design holds the hand of another, how things developed from one period to another. All of these things are massively important. I can't stress enough that doing the things I'm suggesting will create the future for you. All you have to do is read, all you have to do is drive somewhere and look at things. All you have to do is listen to people who know what they're talking about. It's an incredibly easy thing to do, and everything you learn will be of use, whether that's recognising rubbish or genius (you have to be able to do both). But you do have to do what it takes to get there.

What you've read so far might feel a bit like a smack in the face, and you're probably thinking, *That's a pain in the backside. I work full time and I've got five kids. I've got a dog. My leg's fallen off.* Yes, it's difficult, but you can do it. If you want this badly enough, you can find the time. If, on the other hand, you're thinking, *D'you know what – I can't be arsed with that. I can't be bothered. It's not for me. I'm not that interested. I haven't got the time. I don't need to do that. I'm making money trading on eBay.* Fine. Put the book down and walk away, because this life might not be for you.

Everybody thinks they can be an antiques dealer. Believe me, the number of times I've stood in a pub and someone has said, 'Antiques dealer? That's a piece of piss. You just buy it for a pound and sell it for a thousand, don't you?'

And I'm stood there thinking, *My god, you have no idea.*

There's no point continuing the conversation, because it's going nowhere. But they carry on regardless: 'I've seen you on the telly. You buy it for nothing and make a fortune out of it, don't you?'

No, I don't. No one does. That's not how it works. That's not the antiques business – that's just bullshit. Occasionally, and I mean occasionally, you get lucky, but in order to do that you have to put yourself in the way of that luck. You have to be in it to win it. It's the same in any business. That's how the world works.

If you're that person in the pub – grow up. The reality is that we often lose money in our business. And we risk our own money, so when people say that it's easy to make a profit from antiques, they have no idea what they're talking about. They've not been there and they've never done what you're about to do.

There's another one you'll hear all the time, a classic: 'I can do what you do. I can do that. It's easy.'

Really? Can you? Are you sure? You haven't done it, though, have you? You haven't done it, and there's a reason why: because it takes hard work, resilience, time. It takes graft, effort and, above all, love. You've got to love this business if you're going to do it well and make the kind of commitment it takes to be successful.

Dealing antiques is not easy; the amount of time and energy you expend finding things, going to get them, picking them up, moving them around and bringing them to the level they need to be at so you can sell them, can be incredible. Then there's the knowledge you need to do it right, the equipment, the space. None of that's easy – you've got to create it. It's part and parcel of building a business.

Restoration

The art of restoration is another aspect of the business that you really need to be familiar with before you start to buy your first items. If you know nothing at all, one place to begin is YouTube, where there are lots of videos of people restoring all sorts of things – although you do need to be careful, as anyone can post a video and it's important to ensure that the person you're watching is an expert and knows what they're doing.

I'm not necessarily talking about researching the practical side of restoration here, although it does help. For example, say you need a chair to be upholstered, it's good to have a rough idea of the work that will need to be done. The chair will have to be stripped down correctly – there is a way to strip a chair of its upholstery without doing more damage. Then there is a right way to cut the fabric and a specific amount of fabric will be needed for the overlay. And it helps to know what type of nails, what type of horsehair, what type of stuffing, what type of buttons they're going to use.

But you don't personally need to know all the ins and outs of restoring a particular item. What you *do* need to know and understand are the broad facets of the process and what is and what isn't possible. This means you need to know how long the job's going to take, you need to know what methods are going to be used, you need to know what materials will be required and you need to know the cost. You can't go into a restoration process blind – you must know those four things in order to make an informed judgement about whether you can add enough value to justify having the work done.

Also, if you're thinking about having a go at restoring something yourself, I would advise you not to. Are you a fully trained antiques restorer? No? Then it doesn't matter what discipline we're talking about, be it upholstery, French polishing, architectural stoneware – do not touch it. Instead, you need to buddy up with a good restorer. Years ago, an old dealer said to me you need two things in this business: a good restorer and a good accountant.

If you're not an expert – leave it alone. Find the expert, let them make whatever intervention is necessary. It's so important you don't mess with things. If you do the wrong thing, you can wipe off the value in an instant. Just because you can afford to buy something doesn't make you an expert in every aspect. My house is full of unrestored Howard furniture – the arse is falling out of it, but that's the way I'd rather have it. It's not to everybody's taste – some people want things fully restored and that's fine. If a customer wants something restored, you can put them on to a restorer. You might add a small percentage and increase your overall profit. That's something we used to do, but we don't any more, because everyone has a different expectation of how something should look and it's an area that's fraught with problems.

There are a multitude of different disciplines in the field of restoration. If, for example, you're dealing primarily in garden statuary, you need to find someone who can repair composition stone, marble, etc. If you're dealing in wrought or cast iron, you need to find a blacksmith. Talk to these guys and see what they've done in the past. The easiest way is to go through another dealer. Ask for help. Generally, the very best people in each trade don't advertise and they're inundated. You need to befriend them, put yourself on their list of contacts and make sure they're available to you. I'm blessed with some of the best restorers in the business. Neville Morris, for example, is without doubt the best blacksmith in the UK, if not the world. He won blacksmith of the year thirteen years on the trot and the only reason he didn't do fourteen was because he didn't enter and let someone else have a go. He's sixth generation, as good as it gets. He has a natural aptitude. He's brilliant.

Your restorers are essential. You really do need to find the best person you can in that field, as you don't want people who are going to go in ham-fisted. If somebody says they'll do something for you tomorrow, they're generally not worth bothering with. If they've got a waiting list and are not advertising, try and get them to do the work you need. They'll be the best. Once you have a relationship, look after them. Pay them promptly. I pay all my restorers the day I get their invoices. I do the same with my shippers and certainly all my trade contacts. I never let anyone wait for their money. Pay them all on the nail – you're nothing without them in this business.

Every time you buy something that's not quite pristine, you have a choice as to whether to restore it or not. It's up to you and I'd advise you to think about it very carefully. You don't have to restore everything, or even anything at all if you don't want to. Sometimes bringing stock to the market which is completely unrestored but 'right' can be more profitable. For example, I recently sold a wonderful pair of completely untouched chairs, and that was where the value was. I could've had them regilded and reupholstered but that wouldn't have added anything so I sold them in exactly the same condition as I'd bought them. I wouldn't have made any more money if I'd had them worked on. You always ask yourself this question, especially in the early days: will restoration add value? There's no definitive answer. Sometimes it will and sometimes it won't, but you need to ask yourself the question. Restoration can add value. But not restoring can also add value, or at least preserve it. It's about doing the right thing and, once again, it's only really experience that can teach you.

Occasionally, I'll put unrestored items on my website, because some things are more exciting and worth more in their found state. In fact, doing work can sometimes devalue an item. There's nothing wrong with selling something in its raw state. Just give it a clean, or if you've got a chair and it's got horrible fabric on it, take the fabric off (if you're sure you know what you're doing and won't cause any more problems or damage). If you've got an incredible garden statue but the arm's broken off and you don't know how to stick it back on properly, just sell it as is. As I said, there's a certain level of excitement in a found object for some buyers and restorers, and many dealers will want it in that untouched state. You can learn to present something in an unrestored state and make just as much money – without spending any of your own.

The decision to restore or not can therefore be tricky at times. I was very lucky, as I trained in stained glass and was around my father who did restoration for various dealers, working on paintings and clock faces. I was taught 'minimum intervention'. Those two words are invaluable, and you should carry them with you your entire career. Remember, it's all about adding value. Two of my Howard chairs (both falling to pieces) are worth £15,000 – restored they'd be worth £20,000, but it would cost £10,000 to restore them. To restore them would be to lose money, and you're in the business to make a profit, so do your homework. Another thing you need to bear in mind if you are going to restore is the fact that not only are you incurring additional costs, the items are also off the market for a considerable amount of time, and you really can't afford that, especially when you're starting out and haven't built up a financial cushion.

Selling unrestored items when you're at the very bottom of the trade is a very good thing to do because you're not spending additional money, you're creating options for the next person in the chain and you're leaving plenty of profit in the item for them. That next person will probably be more experienced than you and they'll know exactly what to do with it. If you're 100 per cent sure you should have the work done, and you're definitely going to add value and bring something more desirable to the market because of it, do it. But use the very best restorer in the field. If you're not 100 per cent sure, don't do it. It comes down to an instinct, a gut reaction, which will evolve with your experience. Stick to it. You can add your margin by writing a proper description and taking good photographs and offering to help with delivery.

*

Everything I've described in this chapter is an ongoing process and doesn't end. Learning about antiques and doing your research will not end. Meeting new restorers will not end. Going to museums and galleries and National Trust houses to look at things will not end. Collecting auction catalogues will not end. You'll always be learning new things and expanding your knowledge. I'm just giving you some basic nuts and bolts and letting you know the things that have helped me to get to where I am today. But this advice is a starting point. Becoming a better antiques dealer is a lifelong process.

2
BUYING

So, we've established the practical basics of what you're going to need in order to get set up and you have cash in the bank, so now you're ready to buy and that's where you make your money. Read that last part again! If you buy right, you'll sell right. The first step is to go out and buy stock you think you can sell at a profit. This might seem obvious, but it is much more difficult than it sounds; the way you do it is really important.

How to Buy

We're still talking about making those first few inroads into a business you know very little about at the moment, so you're not always going to know what's what. The only way to learn is to start putting into practice the little I've been able to impart so far. I therefore suggest you give yourself a week to buy the stock that will launch your business. You're probably thinking a week's not long enough, but as I will explain in more detail later, moving stock quickly is central to making a profit, so it's best not to hang about when buying your first items. You can do it if you get up early enough and work hard enough, and that means staying out for as long as it takes. That's how it is – it's not for the work-shy. Get in your car, go to every auction house, every dealer, every demolition site. Put adverts in the local press and in local shop windows. If you're going to stand a chance you have to make yourself known to property developers, solicitors, estate agents – anybody who has anything to do with houses. You go round and tell them you want to buy their stuff and you'll pay in cash or by immediate bank transfer. No messing around – you'll do the deal right away. Take what you've bought with you. It's from those sources that you build up your stock.

This isn't dealing. This is buying and, as I said before, your money is made in the buy. This is incredibly important. It's how you get your first bunch of items together and you need to have your heart and soul in each of those pieces. Every one you pick up had better be red-hot, the very best you can buy given your knowledge, budget and experience. You need to be brave. If you do it right, chances are you'll buy something really good straight off the bat.

Discretion

You need to think about how you're going to spend your start-up money, and the worst thing you can do is buy indiscriminately. It happens all the time: someone new to the trade comes in and they splash the cash without fully thinking about what they're doing. An old northern friend of mine used to say, 'Money – it's not for spending!' Think very carefully about the kind of items you want to buy then set yourself an amount to spend on each and try not to deviate too much from it. Use that money wisely. Always remember it's called 'the antiques business'. It's not the antiques game show. It's not the antiques gymkhana or circus – it's the antiques *business*.

The ability to buy the right stock is absolutely critical and the first lesson we all have to learn is discretion. When you're buying you have to be able to look at something and say to yourself 'That's one of the best examples I've seen'. You have to be able to identify this quality for a number of reasons. If it isn't one of the best examples, it's time to do one of the hardest things there is in the antiques business: walk away. Discretion is the number one quality that separates the very best from the very worst. If the item you're looking at doesn't seem right – perhaps it's been tampered with or it might be a reproduction – you should walk away. If there's a tile missing you're going to have a problem selling it. If there's a leg that's been changed, potential buyers will be hesitant. If it's slightly the wrong size, or if it's too low, too high, too wide, too dark, too worn out, you're giving yourself a problem. If there's a question to be answered – don't buy it.

But people do. They think 'Ah there's a quid in that, it's only a little thing, I can get round it.'

Trust me, especially at the beginning of your career, you can't, and you probably won't. No matter how small you think an imperfection is, you're probably not going to fix it because you're not a restorer. You're probably not going to find what's missing. And you're not going to find someone else who's going to put up with it.

If there's something wrong with an item, and it's a glaring problem, you're giving yourself an added headache that will need to be explained to the buyer, making the piece worth less and making the buyer less excited. I always sell all of my stuff with any questions already answered if I can. Is it all original?

Yes. Has it come from a good property? Yes. What year is it? It's that year. What needs doing to it? It needs that done. It's just a simple bang, bang, bang. It gives confidence to the buyer, makes the sale easier and keeps the value up.

For example, if we're talking architectural antiques, go and buy the nicest cast-iron tiled insert you can find. This is where the right research comes in. You need to buy the right size – you don't want one that's too late in period or too small for the age; you don't want one that's reproduction or missing some of the tiles. I could be talking about anything here. It could be stamps, or it could be furniture. The principle relates to anything you're buying and selling.

You must train yourself to buy the things that are right, and do this all of the time. Do not deviate. If you can't find what you were looking for and you come home without having bought anything at all, that's fine. If you go out the next day or the day after that and you don't find anything that hits every single one of the parameters you've set for yourself, that's fine. Keep going until you find the item that does. For me, those parameters fall broadly under the categories of originality, scale, condition and history. Whenever I look at something, I'm thinking, *Has it been altered? Has it been restored? Is it complete? Is it untouched?*

Is the year correct or is it a later reproduction? If you were looking at a nice painting, you might ask yourself, *Has it been overpainted? Has it had a touch up? Has it been cut down from a larger piece? Is it a copy? Is it a print? Has it been reframed? Has it faded?* Whatever chosen subject you're in, you need to have a set of parameters that you work to.

When you do and the item meets those parameters, the sale will be quick and easy. They will see you with different eyes, the right kind of eyes, the ones you want looking at you, the kind of eyes you need if you're going to make it as an antiques dealer. You'll immediately command respect and that's vital. If you approach the business by compromising and tell yourself, 'That's OK. That's close enough. That's nearly there or that'll do,' then you'll be a 'that'll do' type of dealer and that isn't good enough. Well, not for me.

I can hear you asking how you'll know what's authentic and what's reproduction, what's good, what's bad, what's saleable, what's not. The answer is simply knowledge, time on the job and graft. Unfortunately, there's no quick way of obtaining it. Knowledge cannot be gained overnight, which is why so few people really make it in this business. Knowing what is right and wrong ultimately comes down to experience. You've got to kiss a lot of frogs, and you've got to make an awful lot of mistakes. There is an old saying in the antiques trade: 'You pay for your education.' If you buy something wrong, and you can't get rid of it or you lose money on it, you'll never make that mistake again. That's why I always say the best thing to do is buy and sell lots and lots and lots of stuff as quickly as you possibly can. Your learning curve will be exponential. The only way to get experience is to buy things and to make mistakes. The aim is to get to the point that I'm at, where I can look at something from 30 feet away and say, that's wrong. That castor on that left-hand side is a quarter of an inch down, which means it's been changed. That's going to cause me a problem. If I can't solve that problem easily, I'm not buying the piece.

Be brave, and if you make a mistake, get out of it quickly. If I make a mistake, which I still do from time to time, I say to myself, 'It's cost me a thousand quid, but it's probably only worth six hundred. Let's get that six hundred quid back.' I've lost £400, but the problem's gone and I've learnt something and can move on to the next thing. If you don't make mistakes in this business, you will never learn anything.

In your quest for that knowledge it is essential that you handle things, and a great way to do that is to go and work for someone within your chosen field. The very best piece of advice I can offer is that you get yourself a job as a porter at an auction house. There, you'll be handling all sorts of different items for sale and that's the best way of learning the kind of discretion you need to be successful. Other than that you just need to get out there: museums, fairs, auctions, emporiums, old buildings – the world! Open your eyes – a doorknob, a light fitting, fashion, the music industry, cars, all of these will train your eye.

When it comes to buying antique furniture specifically, sit down and really look at what's in front of you. I mean that literally. Sit, don't stand. People tend to stand and look when they buy furniture; you see it all the time, from auction houses to department stores. They stand over the piece when in reality that's not how you or your prospective client is going to view it. It's a small tip, something I learnt a long time ago, but it really does make a difference. When you're standing, you're looking down at the piece and that's fine, but I think it's far better to be at the same level as it. You'll see me do this on *Salvage Hunters* or if we bump into each other at a flea market or fair. I sit down and look because that's the angle from which you'll be looking at it in the house. That's how your buyer will be looking at it when they get it home so you need to see what they see. Every piece of furniture, whether it's functional or decorative, has to sit right in the room and the best way to view that is mostly if you're sitting not standing.

So, how you look at something, from what angle, is an important part of the knowledge. A really important part. You don't need to know everything, but looking at something and saying to yourself, *Yes, that's dead right* is gold dust, and you'll need to acquire that ability in order to buy the very best of something. Go and look, handle things, talk to people, buy things you want to keep yourself if you're restoring an old house or doing a room or buying for a collection. When you buy for yourself, you know what you want and you apply that same knowledge when you're buying an item to sell. Make sure you listen to the voice in your head, that little nagging noise telling you that you shouldn't buy this item for one reason or another. If you look at something and you feel the tiniest seed of doubt then walk away.

There's only one way to obtain the knowledge you need in order to make that decision and that's to go and look at the very best example of something. This can be anything from a door handle to a Picasso. Search out where the best one is then go and look at it. If it's a piece of Regency campaign furniture, go to the V&A museum. Don't look at it for two minutes or five or ten – take a chair, plonk yourself down in front of it and look for an hour. Take a flask and bag of sandwiches if you want, but sit there for as long as it takes. You'll take in the fine lines or some detail, the form, shape, imagination behind it. And make sure you take note of the items that don't hit the mark. If you take as much time studying the worst examples you come across as the best, you'll start to recognise quality.

The other day I bought a chair from an auction in Whitchurch with an estimate of £400. I looked at it and thought, *My god.* From the scale of the leg to the stretcher, to the armrest, to the quality of the carving, to the scale of the backrest, to the rake of the seat, to the wood, to the castors – this was a superior example. I couldn't attend in person on the day of the auction, so I asked for a phone line, and I ended up paying £3,600 for this chair. Somebody else had recognised its quality as well, and we ended up bidding against one another. Out of the thousands of people who had looked at this chair, two of us had recognised its quality and had decided we wanted to buy it. You can only recognise that from looking at the best and worst examples of things. Because I know what the very best looks like, I'll potentially make some money when I sell that chair.

A pair of shoes, a watch, a hat or a piece of furniture will have clues that tell you what is good and what is bad. You have to learn that and the only way of doing so is by getting up close and personal. You have to do it in person. You can look at a thousand different items on the internet but that won't tell you what's good and what is not. You have to walk around a piece, sit and stare at it. You have to see it, feel it from every angle, because:

- You'll understand the scale.
- You'll be able see how fine the workmanship is, the quality and finish.
- You'll pick up the subtleties and nuances: the scale of the frieze, the thickness of the legs, the height of a foot with an inset castor above the carpet.

All these minute details matter, and you must learn to recognise them. It's so important. I'm not trying to brow-beat you here, just pass on what I think is key. The level of knowledge you have will set the benchmark for who you're going to be and you have to start as you mean to continue.

And you can't be indiscriminate in your approach – you have to be strategic. You have to know where you plan to sell what you've bought and if that setting is applicable. Get to know your marketplace. Do that before you go out to buy because, if you're looking to sell in your local area, for example, you need to know what people really want before you make your first purchase. Where I lived in North Wales they wanted slate slab floors, beautiful old oak chimney pieces, stained-glass front doors, large tiled-insert fire grates – that type of thing. On the other hand, if you're in central London they want marble chimney pieces and dog grates. They want quality door furniture. Do your research and set yourself a realistic goal in the area of the antiques world you want to inhabit. These days most of us trade on the internet. There the world is your marketplace and your life as a dealer is much easier. But if you don't want that kind of exposure and would rather stay local, then there's nothing to stop you.

The Magic and Buying What You Love

When you're buying, you might be lucky enough to stumble on that one fantastic piece, but it's unlikely (it does happen, though, and it's an incredible rush when it does). Instead, go out and buy whatever is in your wheelhouse, the things you really want, and not the first things you see where you think you might make a profit. When I started, the plan was to buy architectural antiques as well as architectural salvage. Architectural salvage includes doors, floors, radiators, stonework, slabs – stuff like that, whereas with architectural antiques you're talking fireplaces, lighting, chimney pieces right through to club fenders, stained-glass windows, chimney pots and decorative stonework. That's just an example of what I was into, and the kind of stuff I loved and still do. Decide what's important to you.

Buying things that you love might sound like your heart ruling your head but it's what works in the antiques business. Go with your gut. This will prove to be your greatest asset or your biggest downfall. If you love something you'll have the passion you need and there will always be someone out there who shares that passion and those will be the people you sell to.

Make sure you've done your research then go out and buy something you love, so long as you believe there's a margin in it (more on margin later). That principle applies whether you're selling to someone down the road or someone in Hong Kong or Australia for five quid or fifty thousand. As far as I'm concerned, buying what you love is the fundamental principle of the business. You're not always going to get it right, but you'll never get it right if you don't instantaneously love it. If you love it, the person who made it loved it and the person you bought it from loved it, then hopefully the person you sell it to will love it too. It's your job to make them see it.

To find what you love, you need to 'put yourself in the way of luck', as we say in the trade. You might be the person who picks up a £3,000 dog grate and makes £2,000 on it immediately. Fortune favours the bold, so don't be timid and don't be faint-hearted. Gain as much knowledge as you can and trust your instincts. To be able to do that right from the off is rare – generally it's something that comes with experience. But the really exciting thing about this business is the fact that those items are out there and you might be the one who finds them. That's the thrill – that's what gets the adrenalin pumping, the reason you get up and hit the road every morning. It's the 'magic' that drives this business.

When I talk about the magic, I'm talking about that 'Oh my god!' moment. It's the instinctive reaction *you* have to what might look like an ordinary piece to anyone else but *you* know is something really special because you've studied it, and now all that hard work is paying off and you see what nobody else does. It might be to do with what something is worth but it might not. You can get to a point where what an item costs doesn't matter – that might sound unrealistic when you are just starting out, but stick with me on this one. Twenty grand on a chair? If you're in a position to buy something of that value and you know you can sell it at a profit, the price is irrelevant. Whether it's fifty grand, fifty quid or a fiver makes no difference if the item you're buying has the 'magic'. It's what you're looking for every time you hit the road. It's the gut instinct that kicks in when you find that special something, and it's the ability to recognise it that we all want to acquire.

It's the most exciting part of the job, seeing something in what appears to be a crappy old item stuffed at the back of a shed that nobody else has spotted. It's not about the price. It's about the item. There's a dealer I know whom I'll call D – a very good dealer, one of the best there's ever been in fact – who took me under his wing 20 years ago. Right from the off he told me what happened to him with an older and much more established dealer. D works alone. He doesn't have a van, doesn't have a showroom to speak of really. He has a garage – a very nice one, but it's a garage nonetheless. He's only been using the internet for the last three or four years, but when he sets up at an antiques fair every other dealer sprints to his stand immediately. It's because his ability to spot the magic in an item is better than any of us.

Back in the 1980s, D and this other dealer were in London one night and drove down Kensington Church Street. That was *the* place back then, with antiques dealers from one end of the road to the other. They pulled up outside one particular shop and the older guy told D to look in the window. 'There,' he said. 'That's what you do. That's how you do it. There.' He pointed out a pair of cast-iron Coalbrookdale fern-patterned benches with pale pink paint all fallen off and the wood underneath covered in moss and lichen. 'That's it,' he said. 'That's what we do. I shouldn't need to tell you any more. You either get it or you don't, and I think you do.'

I wasn't there but I could picture the scene in my mind as he was describing it to me. I knew instinctively what he meant: *the magic*; that essential something in a piece that some of us can see – and some will never see.

That magic is the reason you buy what you love. If you don't love something, how can you see the magic? Don't buy anything somebody tries to bully you into taking. Don't buy projects unless you can finish them within a short timescale. Don't buy things that are going to cost a small fortune to restore and you're going to have for months. And don't buy silly things you think will look good in your shop, things you've seen someone buy before for a bit of a laugh. It's not a laugh. It's a business. It really annoys me when people buy silly things and hang them on their wall and then moan that they've got no money. You've got no money because you bought a bloody fibreglass fish and stuck it on your wall because you think that's what antiques dealers do. They don't. Instead, go and buy things that you love, that have the magic and that you're going to be able to turn over. Remember, we are first and foremost dealers not collectors.

Where to Buy

You've established the market you want to work in and that you're going to buy what you love. So who and where are you going to buy from? Antiques can be found in the most unlikely places. There are some obvious ones, like auctions or fairs, but you're also going to buy from other dealers and you're going to buy privately, and there is a roster of skills you need to learn to be able to do so effectively in each setting. Let's start with trade deals.

Buying Dealer to Dealer

Dealer to dealer is the best business you'll ever do, and, in actual fact, it probably makes up the majority of business done in the UK. Items make their way up the tree of dealers until they find their level where someone can sell them to a client or to the general public. Someone below me in the tree might have a really good item but not have access to the market in which it will sell, so they pass it on to me and I sell it, or I pass it further up the tree. Trade deals, as they are known, are done with the least amount of fuss. There's no messing about. If you're buying from a dealer, they give you a price, you either accept it or you don't, and that's it – done and dusted. If you agree the price, you buy it there and then and you take the item away.

There are a few benefits to this model:

- There's an invoice trail, which tells you that the piece is legitimate, correct and that you are

covered from a legal/insurance point of view. That's the boring part.
- If you trust that dealer, you know they'll have been all over the piece, checking it for all of the things you're going to check it for.
- They're going to be honest with you and tell you if anything is wrong with an item, as to withhold this sort of information would be very damaging to their reputation.
- You're building an ongoing relationship that can provide you with business for years to come.

If you're meeting a dealer whom you've never done business with before – maybe you're going to their shop or warehouse, or maybe you're visiting them at their home – there's a way I believe you need to conduct yourself, and it's recognised throughout the antiques business.

First, be prompt – a friend of mine says, 'I'd rather be ten minutes early than one minute late,' which is a very good way of looking at it. So, arrange a time to be there and arrive when you said you would. Don't ring up and tell them you're sorry but you're running late and you'll be there in four hours' time. That's not good enough. You've wasted somebody's day. Generally in this business people are sole traders working on their own, and if they've arranged to see you it means they can't see anyone else. If you agree 11 o'clock be there at five-to, ready to go. I'm terrible at timekeeping but I try very, very hard to make sure I'm never late for an appointment with another antiques dealer.

Second, be upfront. The dealer you're talking to has often held the item in question back so you need to be upfront right away. If you turn up, walk through the door and instantly don't like it, say so. Don't dick about. Tell them. 'I'm really sorry but it isn't for me. Do I owe you anything?'

'No. That's OK.'

You'll part as friends and be able to do business together in the future. Don't spend an hour kicking the thing around, looking at it, wasting the person's time when you know you're not going to buy. I know within a split second of seeing something whether or not I'm going to buy it.

I once bought a pair of chairs on the way to the hotel after we'd finished filming and as soon as I saw them I knew I was going to buy them. It was one of those typical days when I woke to three WhatsApps from a mate of mine who's a dealer in Liverpool. He sent pictures of a load of stuff and, in among it all was a really nice 1870s ash and yew wood desk he'd just got out of a clearance. I asked him how much, and he said £950.

'Yeah, I'll have it.'

I was still in bed at this point, but I'd already made a purchase. At nine o'clock I called an auction house and asked to book a phone line for a set of chairs. With that done I checked my emails – a load of bits and bobs to look at but nothing for me to buy. From there it was my usual breakfast of coffee to go from the first petrol station we passed and on to the filming location, which turned out to be an excellent call, one where I started buying straight away.

Once I was finished there, I went to a dealer I've traded with before. He knew I was going to be in the area and asked me to call in as there were a couple of items he thought I might be interested in. I'd bought one piece off him in the past, a really good painted pine chest of drawers, which cost me £2,400. It was a belter, an absolute scorcher. Having said that, it took me a year to sell and I only made 400 quid. Not a prefect deal but I made some money and it went to a good client. I should have been able to sell it more quickly – it took way longer than it should've done because I probably paid too much in the first place. But sometimes that's how it is – you pay too much money so you just have to wait to sell it and you might not make as much as you hoped. An acceptance of that, as well as the level of patience you're going to need, are a couple of other things you should have if you're going to succeed long term in this business.

Anyway, this dealer had asked me to call in and had sent me a picture of his showroom. In that picture was a pair of gold chairs that dated to about 1840. They jumped out. I knew the moment I saw them I was going to buy them. Instinct borne of over three decades of buying and selling. With me it's visceral. It hits me in the gut and I make my decision immediately. So, I had decided to buy them long before I walked in and asked how much they were. He told me the price for the pair was £3,800.

'Can I see them together?'

'Sure.'

When I arrived, I didn't say anything. I just watched as he put them together. Now, I had a really good look, sitting down so I could see how they would place in a room and checking them out from every angle (like I described previously). I was scrupulous and quick, going over every single detail. I asked him if they'd ever been on the open market and he said he'd bought them at a public auction a year ago but they hadn't been round the houses. He told me they hadn't been online and I knew nobody else had seen them unless they were a trade dealer who'd walked into his warehouse. That was very important. It was about as fresh as you can really hope for in this business, although nothing is ever going to be perfect.

People will sometimes ask you if an item has been through the rooms, which means has it been through loads of auction houses. Or has it been around the world, meaning has it been through 20 dealers' hands? Has it been to the fairs? If you can answer, *No, it came out of a house last week, it's been in the back of my van and only three people have seen it,* that's fresh. And it adds a layer of excitement. If somebody says to you, 'I just got something in and nobody's seen it,' it adds a certain cachet and makes it more likely you'll want it.

This is the reason why a good dealer will have never owned an item once you've bought it from them. Not literally, of course, but in these days of Instagram, Twitter, Facebook, websites and mobile phone images being shared millions of times a second, you don't want people to have seen an item multiple times before. Not for any illegal reason, but because you want to bring something fresh to the market that will excite your client base, and you want to give the next person along the chain the best chance with it.

The paper trail is still there, so if you have a problem with a piece, you can go back to the seller and say, 'I'm very sorry but this thing was stolen 50 years ago,' or 'This piece that is now a sofa was actually an armchair.' It's not about deceiving people. It's for marketing purposes.

So, these chairs I was looking at were about as fresh as you're going to get, but I didn't tell him right away that I was willing to buy the pair at the £3,800 he was asking. They were worth it. I wasn't going to try and knock him down, but I'd try and buy a few more things where there might be some room to improve my margin. I asked him who the chairs were by and when they were made and he told me. I already knew but I wanted to know his opinion because he might have had some more information I wasn't aware of. I still didn't tell him I'd have them. I took a look around the showroom to see what else he had that caught my eye. There were a couple of items – three, in fact: a wonderful marble-topped console table jumped out, and I decided I was having that as well.

'How much is that console?' I asked him.

'Eighteen hundred.'

All right, I'd mull on that. Meantime, there was the most fantastic late George II/early George III mahogany console, which would have been better with a piece of marble on the top but was still a really good thing. It had a tapering leg and a paw foot. It was a great colour – it looked a little bit Irish. Then there was a mirror that looked a bit Chippendale but wasn't – 'inspired by' for sure, but not the real thing. That was £3,200 and the Georgian table £2,800.

'Right,' I said. 'I'm interested in the table and mirror, and I'm interested in the chairs and the marble-topped console. I tell you what, I'll take the chairs at £3,800 as you said.'

'Great.'

It was a lot of money for a pair of chairs you couldn't sit on without a load of restoration, but they were beautiful and they just struck me as something interesting. As far as the marble-topped console table was concerned, £1,800 was a bit toppy, but you don't get offered really good fresh stuff like this every day, so when you do you've got to fill your boots. I told him I'd take the console at the asking price as well – it was an absolute storming thing and I wanted to own it.

'OK,' I said, indicating the mahogany table and the mirror. 'So, that's the chairs and console at full price. I really like these two as well but they're a little bit too much money.' This is how it can work dealer to dealer. I'd already agreed two deals at the price he quoted so he was happy. On top of that I'd told him I was interested in two more. Right now, he was thinking, *Great, we've got a cracking sale going on here, the whole deal is worth £11,600.*

'I want your best price on those two pieces if I take them now,' I said. 'I'm happy to do that but I can't pay full price, as there's some work that needs doing before I can retail them.'

He didn't have to agree to a reduction, but I'd given him an honest account of what I could do. Because of that he did what I hoped he would and knocked 400 quid off the second two items. He was still making money, and I was making money. I paid him there and then, and everyone was happy. That's exactly how it should be. Dealer to dealer. It's straightforward and you leave the door open for future business. The person you're dealing with is happy. You're happy. You've made money. You both feel good – it's the perfect relationship.

Stand On

When it comes to buying and selling dealer to dealer, if it turns out it's not quite what you thought it was or you paid too much, or if you've made a mistake – tough. You shook hands so now you have to lump it. It's called 'standing on' or to 'stand on'. If you say you're having it and you've made a mistake you soak it up – living with your mistakes and learning from them is part of the business. If you buy something that's wrong, you will never make that mistake again. You don't moan, you don't try and wheedle your way out of it. There's nothing worse than somebody coming back and saying: 'Oh, I'm not happy with it now. I've bought it and it's not quite right, it doesn't fit.'

Too bad. You bought it. It's a trade sale. You take your chances. Stand on. I had it recently with somebody who wanted to buy a £7,000 sofa: they hammered and hammered on the price, kept pushing it down until I wasn't making anywhere near what I should've been, but we came to an agreement. I took the money, told them to collect it whenever they wanted and boom, job done. Happy days, right? No. A week later they're on the phone telling me it didn't fit the space and they wanted to send it back. That's not the way it's done. I told them I didn't want to appear rude but it was a trade sale. There was nothing wrong with the sofa and I wasn't prepared to take it back. Not only that, I made it very clear I didn't want to do business with them again.

It happens, although thankfully not that often. This whole business is built on trust but there are a few antiques dealers out there who think they're demigods. They do a few deals, make a few quid and think they're the 'Big I am'. They're not. None of us are. We're in business and part of that business is standing on. If you make a deal and it turns out to be a mistake you just have to accept it and carry on – if you're going to make a loss, make it quick. That's the way it's always been, the way it always should be and it's something you need to learn from the off. Stand by your word. A handshake seals the deal between trade dealers and there is no going back.

Like I said before, we 'chance' our money in this business – there's a risk involved. We pay upfront, on the nail – we don't get credit like a normal retailer does. It's what makes it exciting, what gets you up in the morning. When I first started out 30 years ago there was never any question when it came to standing by your word. Nowadays it seems to have been diluted, some people seem to think they can do whatever they want. They'll get something as cheaply as possible and they don't have respect for the person they're getting it from.

BUYING

As far as I'm concerned this is how a trade sale should work:

> Dealer A: 'I would like to buy your chest of drawers. How much is it?'

> Dealer B: 'I'm asking £2,000 – the trade price is £1,500.

If you're Dealer A, now is the time where you say yes or no. 'That's lovely, I'll take it.' Or 'No thanks, not for me.' There are exceptions; for example, if you're buying multiple items, have spotted work that needs to be done that the vendor hasn't, or there's shipping and logistical costs, like when I was buying the pair of chairs, marble-topped console, mahogany table and mirror from that dealer I knew.

When you buy something, pay as fast as you can and either take it away there and then or arrange to collect it, unless Dealer B offers some sort of delivery. That's the deal done. If there's something wrong with it or if you suddenly decide you don't like it, if it doesn't fit where you want it to go or the client you had in mind is no longer interested, that's too bad. It's the risk you take and if you're not prepared to take that risk, you shouldn't be in this business.

There are no hard and fast rules – we've established that – but, for me at least, there is an accepted code, particularly dealer to dealer. The whinging that goes on now shouldn't happen. It's not the way to behave. A trade sale is a trade sale. You've taken your discount, they've taken a much smaller profit and they've dealt with you directly.

If you behave in the correct way, if you show respect and get this sort of transaction right, you can be buying and selling between a network of dealers for decades. There's one I started working with when I was 23 who I'm still dealing with almost 30 years later. Now and again he'll send me a WhatsApp with a picture of an item he thinks I might be interested in – a chair, for example – and I say yes or no. That's it: a straightforward transaction between two antiques dealers who've spent 30 years working together because the initial transaction was conducted the right way. That first dealer-to-dealer sale established who he was, who I was and we built a buying and selling relationship that's continued. If I don't want what he's offering, I just go: 'Not for me, mate.' And that's the end of the conversation. It should always be that simple. Any other way of doing it is wrong.

These days the business seems to have changed. It's not the way it was. It's changed because, it seems to me, we're in a whinging, whining culture where everybody's a victim and they've got rights which cannot be infringed. Well, this is the antiques business. You can have all the rights you want, and you can whine about this, that and the other, but this is a trade sale. If you're not going to stand on, if you're not going to behave correctly, it will get round the trade like wildfire. Nobody will deal with you. Don't do it. Be a straightforward, stand-up person. There really is no other way.

Buying Privately

When you buy privately from an individual or individuals it's referred to as a 'call' and you're going to make hundreds during your career. Back in the day I had a sign outside my parents' house that said: ANTIQUES BOUGHT AND SOLD. There were no mobiles or email, of course, so I used my parents' landline as a contact: Glan Conwy 454. I also placed an advert in the local paper that said: 'Wanted – Stained Glass & Architectural Antiques, any amount, any condition – cash paid.' People would phone up and my mum would take the calls. She'd write them down on bits of paper for me to deal with when I got home and I'd go through them very carefully. 'Mrs Davies from

Rhos-on-Sea has got some nice old stained glass and a fireplace in her shed. She wants you to go round at four o'clock.' Wonderful. 'Mr Jones from Penrhyn Bay has an old garden bench he wants rid of. He wants you to go round at five.' Brilliant.

This happened all day every day. Sometimes I'd get in and the messages would be ten deep. Back then I was pretty much where you are now with absolutely no experience in this business. There wasn't anyone to learn from about antiques, but I was brought up by my mother and my grandmother who taught me how to behave properly. That's really all you need to do. When you call on someone who's asked you to come round, be polite, be nice, be on time, be smart. Don't be an arse. Smile. Shake the person's hand. Look them in the eye.

Simple, right? Good manners go a long way in life, and they go a hell of a long way in the antiques business. So, I started making calls and pretty quickly I realised I had a bit of a knack for it. I realised I'd found something I was good at, and up until then there really hadn't been very much I could call myself 'good at'. I was confident in what I was doing. It was great. I felt like a superhero. I was going round buying tons of stuff. I was buying so much it was coming out my ears. So, what did it teach me?

No. 1 – Reputation

It's good to buy local, but there are a few pitfalls. If you live in a small town or village, it's very likely that people in the area – whether that is other dealers, auctioneers, collectors or just potential customers – are going to know you. And even if you live in a city, people will get to know you in your area and within the antiques community. So you need to conduct yourself correctly and don't take advantage of people. Be honest and give them a fair price. Yes, a lot of people have very unrealistic expectations when you buy privately, and they'll say, 'Well, I've seen one on *Antiques Roadshow* and it was £5,000, so I want £5,000.' But don't be rude. Just explain that they need to allow you to make a profit and that the price you are quoting them is what it's worth to you and what's realistic in the marketplace today. If someone owns something and thinks it's worth a grand, then they go down the pub and speak to their mates, suddenly they think it's worth five grand. Then I come along and offer them 900 quid. That's why I always say that I'm in the business of disappointing people. Explain the process and make sure there are no hard feelings if you do walk away. This is where honesty, integrity and being professional come in. If you conduct yourself in the wrong way, everyone will know, and you really cannot afford that, because reputation is everything in this business, and you really don't want to get a bad name in your local area.

On the flip side, make sure that when you buy something privately you write down a very accurate description of what you bought and who you bought it from: name, address, telephone number, photograph of the piece in the house, the lot. Make sure you are covered and can prove it was a legitimate purchase. I have a standard deed of transfer document; when I buy something privately, the seller signs it and gets their copy, and I get my copy. It's no good saying, 'I'll give you a fiver and chuck it in the back of the van.' That's cowboy time.

No. 2 – Professionalism

Don't waste people's time, and don't make a nuisance of yourself. If possible, have the means to pay with you as well as a means to take the item away. If they've called you, they want it gone and they want it gone sharpish. If you can get it out the door, they'll be all the more keen to deal with you again in the future. They don't have to think about how they're going to cart it away or deliver it. You're taking care of all that. It's not a hard and fast 'must-do', but it's a bonus, because it shows you're professional.

No. 3 – Respect

Above all be polite. The person you're dealing with might never have sold a single thing in their life – yes, really – so don't patronize them and don't try to be clever. To me and you it's normal – it's what we do every day. Other people get up in the morning, go to their jobs, come home, kiss their husbands or wives, have their tea, watch *Coronation Street* and go to bed. They don't buy and sell things. They stack shelves; they teach in schools; they fix cars; they cut down trees; they paint your walls for you. They don't sell things for a living like we do. So, don't treat them like idiots because they don't know what they're doing. Be open and honest with them. Behave how you would expect someone to behave towards you. It might sound obvious, but you'd be surprised just how many people don't.

*

This is how I do it and I'm not saying you have to do it the same way. You can be as dishonest as you like.

There are people out there who want to rip people off, but that's not my way. Honesty will get you repeat business. It opens more doors, it greases more wheels and it gets you a hell of a lot more house calls – it really does. When I had that sign outside my parents' house, I was the only person in the area doing it bar one other guy who moved away shortly after I got started. That left only me, but I still behaved with integrity. Even more so in fact. Being the only guy to deal with I wanted to make the kind of impression people would remember because you never know how one introduction can lead to another.

For instance, one day this very, very smart Land Rover turned up at my parents' house and a posh local farmer got out, a serious landowner.

'Hello,' he said. 'Are you Drew?'

'Yes.'

'You buy antiques, don't you?'

'I do.'

'Great.' He gave me a piece of ripped-up writing paper. 'Here's the telephone number and address of my farm. Could you come up on Saturday? I've got some things to sell that I'd like to show you.'

'Of course. Delighted. I'll be with you Saturday morning.'

His farm was about ten miles outside Betws-y-Coed, way out in the weeds, really the middle of nowhere. Saturday came around and I drove out in my estate car with roof rack and trailer. I didn't know how much stuff he would have but I thought it was best to be prepared and I was very glad I did. As I drove into the yard I could see there was a big yellow skip and some guys were throwing reeded Regency fire panels into it. These are cast-iron fire backs that reflect the heat, really big ones. They're sought after and they were throwing them on top of each other. I jumped out of the car with my hand up. 'Stop. Stop. Stop. For god's sake, stop.' Thankfully they did, because next to the fire panels, ready to go in the skip, was a pair of massive eighteenth-century lead planters. They were heavily damaged, having been picked up and dumped and driven over by god knows what for god knows how many years, but they were great big ones and I knew that, along with the fire panels, I was going to buy them.

The farmer came over and told me he wanted to set the ground rules before we got started. 'The thing is, if I'm going to sell you anything today I must have total discretion. You can't tell anyone where you got it from. I don't want my name used. I don't want the family's name used and I do not want the property identified. If that's agreed we can come to terms on anything you want to take away.'

'Fine, of course. I understand completely.' We shook hands on that and something in my dense little brain went, *You're onto something here, mate. This is a good thing.*

Ground rules laid, I went round the farm, looking in every outbuilding and every shed and store. I filled my car to the roof with gun cases, boxes full of fishing reels, army uniforms, carpets, furniture, architectural antiques and the lead planters I'd seen when I'd arrived. I didn't spend a great deal of money – a couple of grand in all – but I came away with both the car and trailer brimming, and both the seller and I were happy. To buy that level of stock now would be 20-odd thousand pounds, so that should give you an idea of the kind of quality he was showing me.

As I was leaving he went: 'Remember now, total discretion.'

'Of course. I won't say a word to anyone.'

I left most of the stuff in the car overnight and the next day I carted it around a load of dealers. I went up to Manchester and sold some bits and pieces. I took some items to an antiques fair and sold them there. I went to more dealers and got rid of all bar the lead planters, which I'd earmarked to go into the big sale at Sotheby's South. That was a while away yet and to get them ready I spent an afternoon with a bit of wood and a hammer, knocking them straight enough to sell at auction.

Seven days later I got a phone call. It was the guy from the farm again. 'You've just done a house call for me. Thank you for the money. Thanks for doing it.'

'Well, thank you for the opportunity.'

'I also wanted to speak to you about my cousin. He has a farm near me. Would you be able to go and see him next Saturday?'

'Absolutely. Thank you.'

'Total discretion of course, just like the last time.'

'Of course.'

As I said, I sold much of the stock to other dealers, and saying where the items had come from would've added a lot to the value because provenance and a great house and family name in the antiques business make a huge difference. On top of that it would've given me great kudos, respect within the trade, lots and lots of it. I could do with that. Who couldn't? *Look at me. Look at me. I've got these from this great house and I'm dealing with these kinds of people. How good am I? I really do know what I'm doing, don't I?*

I didn't say any of that – and you shouldn't either. I did exactly what that farmer asked and because I was true to my word he was happy to phone with the address of his cousin. So, the following Saturday I went to his farm which was about five miles from the other one. It wasn't so posh, slightly scruffier I suppose, but again there were some excellent items. I remember one fantastic painted cricket table and a beautiful old tridarn (that's a cabinet or cupboard, traditionally Welsh), along with lots of other stock I knew I could sell to the trade very easily. There was a knackered old Howard slipper chair, some slate fireplaces and a whole stack of other stuff. Again, the guy told me he didn't want anyone knowing where any of it came from and I assured him I would be as discreet as I was with his cousin. I took the stuff away and sold it well and kept my end of the bargain.

The kudos would've been brilliant, enhancing my reputation, but there was no way I was going to break my word to the farmer. That was 29 years ago, and earlier this year I got a call from that same family about another potential clearance. In the years between I've never stopped getting calls: uncles, cousins, aunts, sons and daughters, their friends, and all because I kept my word. Discretion – we talked about it before and it's every bit as important in this context. There are lots of reasons for people to want to remain anonymous, and it's important to respect those reasons. But in this instance, I got the stock, the contacts, the continuity from *not* being the 'Big I am'. It really, really matters. If someone asks you to be discreet then be so.

Financially, these calls with the farmer and his cousin helped me hugely. They enabled me to make contact with the London market and meet a lot of high-end dealers because I had the right things to sell. They took me seriously. We chatted, I showed them what I had and they could see I had a knack for finding really good items. It was the kind of breakthrough I'd been looking for, and it came through that one farmer and his family.

I just did what they asked me to do with no questions. Discreet; straight; honest. It paid dividends. It always pays dividends. It taught me that you don't have to be shouty. You don't have to tell the world how good you are. You don't have to tell people everything that you're doing. Let your work speak for you. By running the business that way I've established the right kind of contacts, people who trust me. I've managed to do business with the kind of dealer I still aspire to be. In fact, I can class the very best dealer in the country, the one I referred to as D earlier, as a close friend because of the way I've conducted myself when we've done business. He's the most low-key, quiet, unassuming guy you'll ever meet. You can spend days with him, weeks, years even, and I have, and you'll know nothing about him, not really. He's got a finger in the pie of every good deal going. He knows about every good deal there's ever been. He knows every dealer worth their salt. He knows exactly how this game works, more so than anybody else I've ever known. But to meet him, to talk to him, you would never know it.

The Three Ds

House calls, or clearances, are a massive part of our trade, so my advice would be to do them the right way. But be mindful of why you've been asked in the first place. Generally, the reason for a sale is one of what I term 'The three Ds': death, divorce or debt. People don't really call you for any other reason. Now and again they might get in touch because they're moving house or clearing out a shed or the garage is too full and they want to get rid of some clutter. They might cut a hedge down and find something underneath. That actually happens more than you might think. In general, though, it's one of the three Ds. So, if someone has died, if a marriage is breaking down or they're in debt, they don't want you turning up and buying their things then shouting about it from the rooftops. Death. Divorce. Debt. Those are private matters, and if you're asked to keep your mouth shut, do so. Keep it shut even if you're not asked to. Do it as a matter of course and you won't get caught out. That's what the best of the best do. It's the right way to work: quiet, steady, not too shouty. Let the quality of your work do all the shouting you need to.

Buying at Fairs

The ability to buy correctly at fairs and markets is absolutely one of the skills you need to have in your roster if you want to make it in the antiques business, and there are a number of important things to keep in mind.

No. 1 – Get ahead of the crowd

Get there early, and I don't mean five minutes before it starts; I mean two or three hours earlier. Get in the queue, get there before the queue starts if you're able to. There was a lovely old trick we used to do back in the day where we'd jump in the back of the dealers' vans before it was light and the fair had started. At the crack of dawn, those of us keen enough would show up and hitch a ride with a stallholder so we'd be there before anyone else. I remember there was one dealer who charged 20 quid for a spot in the back of his van. The way things work, the organisers of the fair let the trade in first (that's the sellers ready to set up) and the buyers arrive a good few hours later. If you were in the back of one of those vans you had the jump on pretty much all the buyers.

I remember going to Ardingly fair, shoving 20 quid through the window of the van to the dealer and climbing in the back where, literally, a collection of the best antiques dealers in Britain had taken a spot. We're all sat there looking at each other and grinning and whispering. 'Hi, how you doing?' 'Hey, how's it going?' It was just the funniest thing imaginable. If that van had blown up, there would have been no more antiques trade in London. Everybody who was anybody was there – this was only about 12 years ago. It still goes on. The only way to win is to get ahead and you'll still find the best dealers squatting in the back of vans waiting to get into antiques fairs.

When I'm at a fair I don't go with a list of things I must buy as I might if it was an auction. There's a constant list in my head anyway. I'm always going to buy if I see some nice table lamps, some good-quality seating or some decent garden statuary. I don't really go with a plan. What I do is move quickly. I mean,

BUYING

really, really quickly. I generally go on my own. There's always somebody who wants to go with me. There's always somebody who's never been to an antiques fair who says: 'Oh, I'd love to go. I've never been to one before. To wander around, looking at this or that, you don't know what you'll find. It'd be amazing. Can I come with you?'

'No.'

'Oh, go on. Can I come with you?'

'No. You can't. This isn't a jolly. It's not a day out. It's business.'

Always remember, this is where you make your money. The buy. I keep banging on about it, I know, but it's important. Buying right is making money. I've said that before. I'll say it again. Buying right is making money, so get there early, get in any way you can. Make sure you're there before anybody else and move quickly. Travel light. I go with literally nothing except cash, card and cheque book. I take a pair of sunglasses and a hat in the summer. I take a torch if it's winter and still dark when I get there.

You're not supposed to buy before a fair officially opens, but all the dealers do it. As soon as you put two dealers together, they're going to start buying and selling. It's like that great old joke about three antiques dealers and a chair washed up on a desert island and all of them make a living. So, buying before the fair opens is frowned upon, but it goes on all over the world – always has done and always will do – and if you want to get in on the action, you need to get there early before all of the good stock is sold.

No. 2 – Act quickly

If you pick something up and have a look at it because you're at the point where you might want to buy it, don't assume it's yours because it's in your hand. Don't faff around because, if it's really good, unscrupulous dealers will buy it while you're still umming and aahing, despite the fact you're holding it. They'll say: 'How much is that thing they're looking at?' The stallholder will give them a price and if it's right, they'll take it. While you're wasting time, they're working.

No. 3 – Be decisive

Don't bother the poor bloody stallholders if you're not going to buy the thing you're looking at, and don't waste their time with inane conversation. 'I like this. How much is it?'

'Fifty quid.'

'Oh, right. I like these. My mum had one of these. I really like it.'

'Really.'

'Yeah, back when I was a kid, we had one at home.'

It's not relevant. If you want it, buy it. If you don't, you've just wasted the stallholder's time. Don't do it. For me, it's a cardinal sin. It really annoys me. Don't pick something up and look at it unless you're half interested in buying it. Don't bother asking for a price unless you're very sure that you're going to buy it. If you think you will, then it's just down to the price and that's the only question you need to be asking, unless there's something about the provenance, for example, that might be relevant. Otherwise, there's no point, especially as most things at a fair are low value – in the £30 to £100 region – and do not justify a lot of time being invested in them.

Generally, if somebody gives me a reasonable price straight off the bat, I will pay it. I'm not going to knock them down £10, £20 or even £30. These poor buggers (and remember, I did it for thirteen years) have got up at four o'clock in the morning. They've loaded their vans in the freezing cold, packed them to the gunwales and driven for hours. They might've slept in the van or some crummy B&B and driven some more, bleary-eyed, and now they're stood there waiting for you to show up and buy something. If it's a reasonable figure at least have the decency to pay them what they ask. Give them their profit because, if you do, they'll be there the next time. They'll remember you. They'll deal with you in a different way if you just say, 'Yeah, I'll have that.' And if you keep doing that every time you see them, it builds up a rapport very quickly. And they won't waste your time with a silly figure if they know you're going to say yes or walk away.

If it's the wrong price, if it's out of the ballpark, I just put it down. To not do that, it has to be exceptional circumstances. For example, you might have a client who wants the item and will pay a premium for it.

For the most part, just buy the item or move on. Another, older, dealer taught me that if you put a piece down, the stallholder will generally shout their best price after you (but not always). Or the next time you ask a price they'll definitely give you the best one there and then with no messing about.

So, be quick, be polite and be decisive. Don't waste people's time. If you buy something, pay for it right away, or say, 'I'll be back later.' This option usually works for both parties, as it means you can both get on with buying and selling, and they'll be more likely to agree to that if you've built up a rapport and they trust you. Also, make sure you get all the relevant paperwork, because you will need it when you come to prepare your stock for sale later. If you do pay on the spot, photograph the item on your phone. Photograph the stall number that's on the floor. Take the dealer's phone number and write down what you've bought. Then move on to the next stall and collect your item later. Keep doing that and make sure you've got the means to take everything you buy away. It might seem obvious but not everyone does it. If you pay for something and the dealer knows you can take it away that day, you'll get the best price straight away. You're solving two problems. They're getting their money and the item is gone. That's the business. It's the most basic thing but it's a tool you can use at fairs, privately and with dealers. Just tell them you'll take it away there and then and you'll get the best price, I guarantee it.

Matching Pairs

The other situation in which I might overpay for something is if I'm marrying an item with something else; for example, to make a pair of bedside lamps. If I've got a really good one that's worth £500 and I see another one that is £600, I might buy it so that I can put the two together. As a pair, their value increases to £1,500.

Matching pieces up can be hugely profitable. Pairs are really saleable, so bear this in mind when you start out buying. Pairs don't just double the money, they increase exponentially. Say one's worth five pounds – if you put another with it, it's not worth ten, it's actually worth twenty. That's how it works – the value goes up and up. It can go on and on, particularly with chairs – a pair of chairs is way more valuable than one on its own.

To give you an example, I've just matched a couple of Indian-made tables in the shape of camels. Each is about three-foot tall with an octagonal top . A standing camel forming a table, particularly one that's well carved, is not something you see every day, and they're very expensive. The other day I saw one at a dealer pal of mine's place in the Cotswolds. As soon as I saw it I thought, *God, I love that. It's a belter.* I'd missed one in the past and have a really good miniature in my house, but nothing on this scale. I loved it – the carvings were exceptional. My pal was asking £7,000 and offered it to me trade at £5,800. It wasn't perfect but the faults were ones I could live with. I thought the price was pretty good because, even with the small faults, it was definitely worth £8,000. I was about to buy it there and then, but then I changed my mind and decided to go away and think about it. Why? I don't know.

The next day we were filming with another mate of mine in Wiltshire. We were on set all day and finally I got around to asking where the loo was. He pointed me through a set of doors but I went through the wrong one and instead of the loo, I found myself in his storage facility. Right there in front of me was the matching bloody camel table. It was a little bit lighter in colour, a bit more faded and it was missing its head. I went to find my mate and asked him how much he wanted.

'It's £1,350. I've got a block of wood I can look out, the right wood to make the head from. I'll chuck that in for you.'

'Great,' I said. 'I'll have it.'

I immediately rang the dealer in the Cotswolds and asked him for the measurements of the other table. He gave them to me over the phone and they matched the one I was looking at. It was £1,350 for the headless one, and I bought the other one over the phone at £5,800, so I was in for £7,150 on two original camel tables. It was a near complete pair and I found a guy who said he would charge me £1,500 to carve the head, bringing the total to £8,650. Now, one on its own is worth £8,000, but to the right buyer a pair is worth £20,000. See what I mean about the value? Instead of two fetching £16,000 they could bring another £4,000 in profit.

There's something else to consider as well – it's not just the monetary value you're adding to. A pair will be extraordinarily well received by other dealers and more saleable to decorators. People will talk about them; people will be annoyed that they didn't find them and you'll have that sense of joy you get when you're able to put two fantastic items together. Be they two nice anglepoise lamps, a pair of club fenders or leather chairs, a couple of football shirts or motorbikes – it doesn't matter: pairing things is a lot of fun and percentage-wise you're going to make a lot more money.

No. 4 – Stand your ground

If you buy something at a fair, that's it. There's no comeback. There's no whinging. There's no changing your mind, which is why you don't handle an item if you're not seriously going to buy it. If you do buy it, it's yours. As I've said before, you've got to 'stand on' and if there's a problem afterwards it's your problem, not theirs. But it goes both ways. Most dealers abide by this code, but there are a few who might try to mess you around. It's happened to me. There are three dealers I can think of who I wish would disappear because they give the trade a bad name.

About 25 years ago I bought a stone horse, a really good one, from one of them at a fair. I paid them the 200 quid they were asking and went back later to pick it up. When I made the purchase there was just the one guy on the stall. We shook hands and I parted with the money. When I went back there wasn't one guy but three and the guy I dealt with goes: 'Sorry, mate. We got the price wrong. We want more money.'

I looked at him. I looked at the other two backing him up, trying to muscle me. No, no, no, this wasn't going to happen. I stood there in front of them and called the fair organiser on my phone. I looked the first guy in the eye. 'That's mine,' I said. 'You don't own it any more. I bought it. It belongs to me. I'm not paying you any more money.' I was bricking myself with three of them and one of me. I thought they were going to give me a kicking. But I kept on. 'Not only am I not paying you any more, you're going to put it in the back of my car for me.'

The fair organiser was on his way with security and I just stood there waiting. It took about ten minutes but I made them put the stone horse in the back of my car. I remember thinking, *Don't you dare do that to me. Who the hell do you think you are?* I stood my ground. I had to. You can't let someone change the rules when a deal has been done. That has no place in the antiques business. It happens – not very often, but it's not unheard of. There are some thugs out there. Not as many as there used to be, but they exist, so be mindful.

*

So, that's fairs. I'm usually gone before most of the public get there. I arrive early, do what I need to then meet up with some mates and have a cup of coffee and a bacon sarnie. I'm typically on my way home by 9am. I don't get chatting with people on the way round – I just keep moving.

Go Against the Flow

People always tend to turn the same way when they go into a fair. I don't know why, but that's the way it seems to go. I don't. I go against the flow. There can be hundreds of stalls and you need to visit every single one. I do that once, then I turn round and go back the way I've come – that way I see every stall a second time. I do that just in case I've missed something. When you arrive that early, people are still emptying their vans so their best stuff might not be on show when you pass the first time. Equally, as they sell they'll have more space on their pitch and they'll be unloading more stock. You don't know what's going to be there. What they consider their best pieces might not be what you think. Not every dealer is as an expert – sometimes there's a massive gulf in knowledge. Which is why you read, it's why you handle things, it's why you immerse yourself in it. Do that and you might just know more than the dealer selling the particular item you want. You don't want to rip people off, but if a dealer doesn't know what they've got, then they haven't done their homework properly. That's their problem, not yours. All you're doing is applying your knowledge.

Buying at Auction

When I first started out, I was in awe of auctions. Buying at an auction was one of the most terrifying things to do – well, I thought so – but I knew it was an integral part of the antiques business so I had to jump right in. I was 18. I knew bugger-all but I turned up at Ball & Boyd's auction house in Llandudno. I had no clue what to do. I'd never bid on anything in my life. I wanted to go but I wasn't sure I wanted to buy anything. I had no way of selling anything. Being honest with you, it was a rufty-tufty old place at the back of Maddoc's Street. The auction is long gone but the building is still there and my mate Jim (who's a dealer) is based there now.

Anyway, I walked in, wandered around and spotted a couple of mirrors. I thought, *Well, I know a little about mirrors*, because I was on a YTS (youth training scheme) restoring stained-glass windows at that time. I told myself I'd handled mirrors before so I probably knew enough to buy some and somehow I'd sell them even though I had no idea what I was doing. So, these two really crappy mirrors came up – overmantel ones from the late 1940s mounted on a bit of old plywood. Absolute rubbish, but I stuck my hand up with no clue what was going on. I'd done none of the preparation you have to do if you're going to bid in an auction. I hadn't worked out how much I was prepared to pay for them or how much was too much. I hadn't worked out a profit margin. I had no idea how I was going to take them away or how to pay. I didn't know where I was going to sell them. I was just desperate to learn how to buy at auction.

Talk about making a mess of it. Now, I wouldn't pay a pound for them. Back then, 29 or 30 years ago, I paid 45 quid. Two ropey old mirrors and the auctioneer was all over me. He was on my case. He told me to hurry up. He said: 'Is that your best bid? That's not enough. You can do better than that. Don't come here messing me about.' He was doing this in front of about 200 people. It was horrible. I didn't know what to do. He scared the bejesus out of me. He wouldn't let up. He just went at me. There was no reason for it. I just thought, *You bastard. You're making me feel really small here.* I had no money. I was on the YTS for god's sake and he's laying in to me like there's no tomorrow. I was bullied into the buy and bought them for 45 quid – more than they were worth. I got them back, put them in the shed with all my other little treasures and I remember thinking: *What the hell am I going to do with them?* In the end I think we cut them up for spares in restorations.

It was a lesson learnt the hard way. An awful way to get into the world of antiques auctions. But I learnt my lesson, and when I went to my second auction, I got the items I wanted for exactly the amount I wanted to pay for them. I took them away, sold them and made some money. I'd worked out that if I put them in the back of the car and drove them round some antiques dealers, I could sell them for a decent profit. Since then I've learnt to love the auction house.

Auctions haven't changed, and to the newcomer they can be intimidating and scary. They were to me at first, but not any more. What I'm trying to say is – don't just turn up like I did. Don't be a rabbit in the headlights, because you will get run over. Go armed. Have a plan. You don't go into battle without a helmet or a gun, you don't go without a map and an idea of who you're shooting at. You've got to have a plan. Now, I can walk into any auction without having seen something in advance and I'm still able to buy – 30 years of experience has given me that confidence. But if you go to buy from an auction when you're just starting out, make sure you're prepared. Make sure you've done your due diligence.

There was a great dealer I knew in North Wales called Frankie Robinson. Unfortunately, he's not with us any longer, but he was a really nice guy and the biggest dealer in our area. He was a friend of my father who used to do all the signwriting on the side of his vans. Frankie was a grafter. He was always doing house clearances and he was incredibly knowledgeable. He'd walk into an auction where I'd be stuck in a corner trying to keep out of everybody's way, scared witless, and he'd be there with a mobile phone to his ear and his hand up. He'd be talking to somebody on the phone and would keep his left hand up until he'd bought the lot he was bidding on. It didn't matter what it was. It didn't matter if it was five pounds, fifty pounds, five hundred – he kept his hand up. That was Frankie. That's who he was. 'I'm here now. I'm in charge. This is how it goes.'

Watching him, seeing how he worked, gave me a lot of confidence. I could see how he was respected. I could see how he controlled what went on in that auction house. If he wanted an item, he got it. He didn't ride roughshod – he just kept his hand up. He was generous, straight and fair. This was the late 1980s and early 1990s, and he was the only dealer in our area I had any time for. He was very kind to me. I'll never forget how, when I lost my job in my early twenties and had to go self-employed, he rang me and asked me to come to his warehouse. I'd done a bit of restoration work for him so we knew each other reasonably well and I was keen to see what he wanted. He told me to be there at two o'clock on such-and-such a day so I made sure I was five minutes early.

'Hi, Frankie; what can I do for you?' I was thinking he had some restoration work he wanted me to do for him. He didn't. He gave me a piece of paper.

'Here's this man's telephone number. Here's his name and address. He lives just outside Chester. Ring him up, go over there with a van next Saturday and give him £1,500 for everything he's got. I'm doing you a favour.'

I took the paper, thinking, *Wow. Amazing. Thank you.* So I rang the guy, told him I'd been given his number by Frankie and could I come over next Saturday.

'Yeah,' he said. 'That's fine. That's great. I'll see you then.'

A week later I turned up at the address on time in a van with my father to help me. I was driving a knackered old Volkswagen van, and my dad was in a 4x4 with a trailer and roof rack. The guy showed me a garage stuffed to the rafters with architectural salvage: carvings, doors, sinks, panelling and fireplaces. There was nothing incredible, but it was good, all of it. I had a look round then turned to the owner and asked him if £1,500 would buy it.

He went: 'Yeah, that's exactly the figure I was thinking.'

I paid him, took everything away and made money out of it. I'll always be grateful to Frankie for that. It was a nice thing to do. He made a friend of me. He gave me a load of confidence. He let me make a profit and from then until the day he died, he never lost my respect. I looked after him as he'd looked after me. If I was clearing a house and came across something I thought would be right for him, I gave it to him gratis. If anyone asked me to do a clearance locally that I couldn't manage, I would always phone Frankie, because he had done me a favour when he didn't need to, and he'd shown me how it was done when it came to buying at auction.

If you want to be a dealer, at some point you're going to have to buy from auctions, and you know from my initial experience how not to do it. Now, decades later, I revel in that environment, so what have I learnt that helped me to navigate the world of auctions successfully?

No. 1 – Research

Get online or get a catalogue and look at the pieces you're interested in as soon as you can. Make sure you do this way before the auction starts or you're likely to wind up paying too much, like I did in Llandudno. Pick the things that you want and do your homework on them.

No. 2 – Plan

Work out what you think you can get for each item. Put those parameters down on paper then work out how much you need to pay for them. Decide on your maximum bid and work out what your costs are on top. Write it down and don't deviate. Stick to it. The money is made in the buy, remember?

No. 3 – Visit the auction house

This is the one thing I would recommend above everything else: if you're really interested in something, go and look at it in person – don't just buy from the catalogue. Yes, I know Edinburgh's a long way. Yes, I know Norfolk is. It doesn't matter. If you're really interested in something, it's going to cost you. Go and look. Do that for lots of reasons. In the flesh, you'll be able to tell if it's been repainted. Has it been repaired? Has it been damaged? If it has, how much work will it take to restore? I also like to see the true scale of an item. I want to be able to look at it and think, *That's really gutsy. It's bigger than I thought, the top's a little bit thicker, it's a better colour*. Or the reverse can be true. *It's actually not as good as I thought. It's not as thick, the colour's not up there where I want it to be.*

It's really important to look physically, but do it quietly. You don't need to go with a song and dance. Go in, nice and quiet; study the piece you're interested in and get to grips with it properly.

If you can't get to the auction for some reason and are still determined to buy, you can ask for a condition report. Every auction house should (and most will) give you a condition report for free. You ring up and tell them you're interested in that chair with such and such a lot number, can they give you a condition report please? They'll come back (sometimes on the phone) and give you a complete breakdown. The back leg's come off and been stuck back on, the seat's been badly reupholstered and it's got staples all over the back. It's had some repainting and the castors don't match.

Now you know enough to walk away. Now you know exactly what's what and if you still decide you want to buy, it's going to be a lot cheaper. If you don't do that, if you only look online, you're not going to know that the £400 chair is actually a £100 chair. You might pay too much and get stuck with it. So, whenever you possibly can, go and look at the items you want to buy. It's another golden rule: view them up close. Don't be lazy – never be outworked.

No. 4 – Don't improvise

Stick to your price. Don't get over-excited. Don't get bidder's fever, don't have your arm flapping up and down like one of those Japanese waving lucky cats. Stick to your price. I repeat, and I'll continue to repeat: your money is made in the buy. Discretion, the ability to see what's really what so you can walk away if you have to, is vital here. It's also useful to list items in order of priority, and price them to sell then price them to buy. I always look at the worst-case scenario: getting rid of items at cost value if they don't sell.

No. 5 – Be discreet

If you buy an item and are able to take it there and then, do so. Don't hang around. Don't make a song and dance. Get it away immediately. You'd be surprised how much posturing goes on in the antiques business. There's a lot of back-slapping, a lot of 'Look at me. Look at me.' There's a lot of the 'Big I am'. Avoid it. You don't need it. What you need to do is quietly go about your business. I've said before this isn't a circus, and it's not for public entertainment – it's a business. The successful people, those who last a lifetime, never forget this. We're not in it for fun, even though it's there. We love it for sure, but we're in business.

No. 6 – Trawl for bargains

The other thing I like to do at auctions (and you can only do this if you're there on the day of the auction) is watch what's going through that's getting no interest. You've no idea what this might be at the outset but there's always something. You'd be amazed at what goes through. I've lost count of the times I've sat there and thought, *That's going for nothing. It's a great thing. It should be fetching decent money.* For some reason it's not selling but they want rid, so it's knocked down to 20 quid. Generally, by this point, the auction house doesn't care what the item sells for, they just want it sold. It's in their way until they're rid of it. If they sell it for anything, they're making money. Remember, they've not paid for it and they've not paid to restore it – they've photographed it and they're stood there selling it. That's all they have to do.

If you're in the room and stuff is going unsold, you can get some absolutely storming bargains after the sale if you talk to the auctioneer. There are dealers who specialise in these things, the items no one else seems to want. Years ago I nicknamed them 'trawlers'. You find them at every auction. They're hanging around. They know the auctioneer and they've viewed every piece being sold. They did that at the last auction and they'll be there at the next, 'trawling' through the stock with an eye for picking up the stuff nobody wants in the hope they'll come across that bargain. They're always around and can be relied upon to, quite literally, pick up the pieces. If something doesn't make it through one auction, it's there at the next. It still doesn't go. It has to go. It's bloody well in the way. That's where you come in if you're the trawler. The lot will come up and the auctioneer will look your way. No more than a glance and it might be an item worth £100 that didn't sell at previous auctions. The auctioneer will look your way. 'Twenty pounds?'

'Yep.'

Bish-bash-bosh – he knocks it down to you. You've got yourself a bargain and this could go on all day. It's really, really useful to you – it's another way of acquiring stock very cheaply – and to the auction house – remember, the auctioneer only gets paid when an item is sold, and he needs space for the next auction.

I've been that trawler on more than one occasion and I'll undoubtedly be so again. I have a huge amount of respect for those guys because it's a hard, if potentially profitable, way to work in this business. I remember an auction in Norfolk about 15 years ago when every time something didn't sell, the auctioneer would glance at an unobtrusive-looking guy in the corner and go, 'Twenty quid?'

The guy would nod and they'd move on to the next item. By the end of the auction that bloke had enough stock to fill his van and he'd paid next to nothing for it. It wasn't the best stuff, but it wasn't the worst either and he'd paid way under the estimate for every single item. He had as much wriggle room as he wanted and a load of stock to either sell at fairs or ferry between other dealers. He'd trawled the depths, spending next to no money, so he could sell this vanload very cheaply. If you've got no money, it's a nice way of getting into the business. Take lower-end stuff that you might normally avoid, then spend a little time on it. Give it a clean. Give it a polish. Fix what needs to be fixing. Put it in the back of your van, drive it to a fair and see what you can do to get rid of it.

*

Auctions are fraught with dangers and you must learn to negotiate them and buy properly. It's very, very important, because the auction is one of your prime sources of stock. It's where you can really add to your inventory if you do your homework and learn to buy properly. You need to get it right and that's not always possible for a number of reasons, though those will mostly be of your own making.

I've made huge mistakes, plenty of them, but one of the worst was at an auction in Chester. The old Bonhams place used to have a monthly or bi-monthly sale of decorative antiques with an architectural and garden section. On this occasion I got the catalogue through the post and, *Hello – there's a pair of late-nineteenth-century Japanese bronze cranes*. I wanted them. They were nicely patinated, just the sort of thing you'd stick in your garden as ornamental decoration and they'd look the business. They were popular, with lots and lots of copies around. You could also buy them brand new and they were excellent. But these were the real thing, going for copy money, and you might be fooled into thinking they were copies. I recognised them for what they were and I didn't come across them very often. Boom. I was having them. Chester's right on my doorstep and I asked myself if I needed to view them. 'Naw, there's no need. I know what I'm looking at. These are the real deal. I'll just fly down there and buy them.'

So, I was going to buy without viewing and that was my first mistake. My second was not booking a phone line. On top of that, I hadn't asked for a condition report; had I done, I wouldn't have cocked the whole thing up completely. No due diligence whatsoever, and I wasn't new to the trade. I wasn't wet behind the ears; I was a fully fledged antiques dealer. At this point in my career I was also overconfident – another big mistake, one I've since rectified (hopefully). This was about 2000 and I should've known better. So, no view, no phone line and no condition report.

I was also running late, another crime – never be late for an auction. It could cost you. It did me. But I thought I knew what I was looking at so I jumped in my Mercedes estate and left for Chester. By now I'd had the car a while and it was a bit clapped out, but I was still a young man and it was a very nice vehicle to look at. It was quick, and I like to drive cars quickly, and because I was behind schedule, I was belting along. There's no excuse for being late, but I'd worked out roughly when the cranes were coming up. I was flying down the A55, absolutely gunning it, when I saw blue lights flashing in my rear-view mirror.

Oh, for god's sake. That's the last thing I need. I was already late and I had to get the cranes – there was a £1,000 profit in the pair, easy. I knew I would turn them around in no time. The sun was shining, garden stuff, wallop. I know what I'm doing. Look at me. Look at me.

So, anyway, the police pulled me over and one of them came up to the window. 'We've just clocked you at 101 miles an hour. That's your licence gone, mate.' *Bugger. I can't afford that. I can't afford to lose my licence.* 'Today's your lucky day, though. I don't know why but I'm going to do you a favour.'

Magic words. 'Really? You're kidding. Thank you.'

'I won't do you for the 101. I'll do you at 95 and that way you won't lose your licence.' He took a step back to have a look at the Mercedes. 'Why are you driving this car?'

'It's mine.'

He looked me up and down. 'I don't believe you.'

'It's my car. Really. I'm an antiques dealer and I'm going to Bonhams to buy some stock. I'm late, that's why I was speeding.'

He accepted that, sat me in the back of the police car and took ages to give me the ticket.

I was now later than late. I was losing time but at least back then you could still use your phone in the car without getting nicked. Dangerous, I know, but I had no choice. The cranes would be coming up and I had to get a phone line because I'd never make it to the auction house in time now. I got going again, jumped on my phone, rang Bonhams and said: 'You've got a pair of cranes coming up, can I have a phone line, please?'

'You're just in time. We're two lots away from them.'

Thank god. I'm all right. I've got the phone line.

The cranes came up and the bids were £100, £110, £120, £130, £140. At that price they were knocked down to me. I thought: *Oh my good god! I've just rung the bell. I'm the best antiques dealer in the whole world ever.* I hadn't viewed the cranes, but I still managed to get them cheap. Happy days, right? Wrong.

I was only 15 minutes away so I carried on, got to the auction house, parked the Merc and sauntered in.

'Hi, I've come to pick up the two cranes. Car's outside. I'll settle up now and take them with me.' I paid for them, including the tax, then went up to collect them when the auctioneer spotted me.

'A'right, Drew. What're you doing?'

'I've come to pick these up.' I nodded to the ornamental bronze cranes.

'They're not yours.'

'What do you mean? I phone bid just now. I bought them.'

He was shaking his head. 'No, you didn't. You might've bought a couple of cranes but it wasn't those ones.'

'What're you talking about? I just bid on the phone for a pair of cranes. I've settled up. I'm here to take them away.'

'A pair of cranes.' He indicated the two I wanted. 'It's not them. It's those over there.' He pointed to a small pair of brass cranes about five inches tall that your gran would've had on her fireplace in the 1970s. Crap. Rubbish. Junk. Reality hit. I couldn't believe it. What a muck-up. I picked them up. I looked at them and just laughed. I'd paid for them. There was nothing I could do. I couldn't complain. Someone else had the ones I wanted and all because I hadn't done my due diligence. I hadn't viewed the sale and I hadn't asked for a condition report. I hadn't brought the catalogue with me. I hadn't written the lot number down. I was trying to be a smart arse and it had cost me lost profit plus three points.

I showed them to the auctioneer and porters and we all had a good laugh. I'd been lucky not to lose my driving licence – I was looking at a fine and three points. When I got back to the warehouse I threw the cranes in the pile for metal recycling. A whole series of mistakes when I should've known better. I did know better – I just didn't do it. It was incredibly stupid. It was down to being lazy and cocky and thinking I knew better than the lessons the business had taught me. I've never forgotten and I never will. I will never make the same mistake again. I'll never be that arrogant. Not only did I get a speeding ticket, when you added in commission and tax, I spent nearly £200 on something I ended up weighing in for scrap – I certainly didn't make a £1,000 profit. The way I looked at it, I came out with a £1,000 loss because I'd messed up completely.

It was my own fault. I ignored everything I'd learnt about buying at auction and since that day I've always done my due diligence. That is until recently. I wasn't in a position to do it because of too tight a schedule, but this time I bought the right thing at the right price because I made a call to make sure I really did know what I was looking at. Our local auction house had four chairs with an estimate of £30 apiece. A mate of mine rang and asked if I'd been on the sale room website. He told me to take a look at three Pugin revival dining chairs and one carver. 'Three diners and a carver, Drew.'

I was like: 'Right, OK. Gotcha.' So I got on the phone and booked a line for 10.30. I bought the four chairs for £280. I did none of the due diligence I'm suggesting you do, but I took a chance. I wouldn't have done that if my mate hadn't rung me up and told me what they were. Because he did, he owned half. When I sold them, I'd take my £280 back but the profit would be split 50-50. You can only do something like that when you've been in the business long enough to have mates in the trade whom you trust. Until then, even then, the very best thing you can do when it comes to auctions is follow the advice informed by my own bitter experience that I've covered here.

3
SELLING

Selling is an art form. Some people are naturals, and some people find it really difficult. But there's absolutely no reason why you can't learn to do it well if you adhere to some simple advice.

Preparing Your Stock for Sale

This doesn't just fall into one category: there's preparing stock for sale at a flea market or antiques fair open to the general public; there's preparing stock for sale at an auction; there's preparing stock for sale at a trade fair; and there's preparing stock to sell via retail. All of these have subtle nuances but we'll concentrate on selling to the public, which is where you get the maximum price for what you're selling.

No. 1 – Inspect your stock

Check the items you're selling very carefully. For example, if you're taking something for sale at an antiques fair in the back of your van make sure it's as it should be. If it's a chest of drawers from a house clearance, check the drawers for old pairs of knickers or socks. There have been. There will be. I've seen it. Whatever is in there, get rid of it.

No. 2 – Problem solve

If it's a chest of drawers, make sure all the drawers run. If it's got locks, try and get them working. If the keys are missing, try and get some. If it's got handles, at least ensure they match. If it's chairs, clean them. Make sure they've got the right castors. If there's one missing, source a replacement and put it on before you come to sell it. It's basic stuff that will make a difference to the price you end up getting. These simple things are often missed or forgotten, and sometimes people just don't want to bother. Go the extra mile and give yourself the best chance. Solve the problems you can see with each item. The more problems you solve the easier and quicker the item is to sell and the more money you will potentially get for it. Remember what we said about seeking out the best? Well, make sure that best is as good as it can be. I always like whatever I'm selling to be a 'no-question piece'. By that I mean remove all possible problems. It makes a hell of a difference.

There will always be questions about the pieces you're offering, of course there will. People will ask you about a chair or campaign chest, a piece of garden statuary. They'll want to know as much as possible so make sure you've done any research you need to.

'Is there anything you can tell me about it?'

'Well, it's a particularly good original piece. It's slightly bigger than normal. The colour's what caught my eye. It has been reupholstered in the past, probably three or four decades ago. It's back to the kind of condition it should be given its age. It's ready to go. You won't have to do anything to it.' And so on, and so on.

All positives. All the problems have been solved already. A no-question piece. You've laid the groundwork for the easiest sale you can hope for.

If, on the other hand, you don't solve the problems and hear yourself saying: 'Well, it's a great piece but there's a castor missing.' 'There is a stain on it.' 'The drawer doesn't run right.' 'That lock's stuck so I can't get the smaller drawer open.' These are all obstacles you need to have addressed before you try to sell it. It's rudimentary stuff but it gets ignored and there's no need for it. The business is hard enough without making it any harder for yourself. The simple, obvious things that get overlooked never cease to amaze me. It's just lazy. I know you've things to do. I know the kids need feeding and the dog needs walking. I know. It's the same for all of us. Make the time. It'll make your life easier. If you haven't got time to prepare an item properly right now, then don't try and sell it until you do. If you go to buy a car and when you get there, the tyres are flat and there's no fuel in it, you're going to lose confidence in the seller and you're not going to buy it, are you? If the seller pumps the tyres up and puts petrol in, you're much more likely to buy it. You wouldn't buy a car with flat tyres so why would you buy a chair with a castor missing? It's the basics of selling something. Take the problem away. It's not rocket science.

Set Your Price

Next you need to decide on a selling price. This is going to depend on whether you're selling to the trade or to the public. Say the price a member of the public would need to pay for something is £100, a trade price would be between 10 and 20 per cent less. If you want to give more of a discount, you can. If you want to give less, you can. It's your prerogative. In the past, dealers just used to say, 'What's your "best" on that?' It was a slang term used just in the antiques trade, but now there are so many antiques programmes on TV, everyone asks you for your best price. So, the meaning of that word in the industry has largely been lost.

You are under no obligation whatsoever to give a trade price, but dealers will always ask for one, and if I were you, I'd begin selling to the trade as soon as possible, because that will get you known, and your reputation within the trade is going to be all important.

More generally, say you paid £1,000 for a nice little chimney piece and you think you've seen one just like it somewhere for £10,000. Don't get carried away. You might have done – it's possible, but unlikely. You've probably seen something similar that's five times larger, from a better house, and it was eighteenth century not nineteenth. Do your homework because if you set the wrong price you're going to look like an idiot and you'll have the item for ages and get sick of it. Ignore what you see on the internet.

If you have something good – perhaps a crystal chandelier, for example – that you bought for £500, you could go online and find crystal chandeliers on websites all over the world with price tags of £500, £3,000, £5,000, £25,000. Those items might look ostensibly the same, but the chances are they are superior examples, as it's unlikely you would have got your hands on a truly great one for £500, although not impossible. This is a mistake I see people making every day. Also, there are different micro markets in different places, and just because a crystal chandelier would sell for that somewhere else, doesn't mean it would in your neck of the woods too. And you have to watch out for one-off auction results in which the prices were inflated for unknown reasons. There is nothing worse than somebody saying I saw something like that on the telly and it went for £25,000, so I want £25,000 for mine. That's not how it works. If you bought yours for £500 and somebody offers you £600, take it. Yes, do your due diligence and make sure that yours isn't something incredible. But once you've done that, put a profit on it and move it. And do that as many times as you possibly can in a day and keep it going. Keep the wheel turning.

Every now and again you'll get something exceptional that has got a really big profit in it. But the size of that profit will depend on where you are in the pecking order of the antiques business, and the knowledge and contacts you have. If a London dealer is going to price something at £15,000, it's probably worth it for them to buy it off you for about £3,000 or £4,000. This is because their costs are extremely high, and they've put themselves in London in a very expensive shop to garner trade from very wealthy, knowledgeable people. That's where their profit comes from, and you need to allow them to have it. And don't think just because they're charging £15,000 that's what they're going to get. They'll probably get nearer to £12,500.

When you start out, you won't have those high-end customers, and you won't be in the position to take on those large overheads. You just need a sale and to make a decent profit, and a good return from a piece that cost you a lot less is still excellent business, even if it will end up going for much more further up the chain. But that is not your concern. Take the sale and never look at what the next dealer is selling it for. That's the worst thing you can do. Never regret a sale. Did you make a profit? If you did, great. Move on and do it again. And hopefully the buyer will sell it and come back to you for more. If they've made a profit, they'll understand that you know how to play the game and want to deal with you again. This is the basis of the whole business and something you should work towards and never ignore.

If you want to 'grocer', you can. That's what a lot of dealers do and they never deviate from it. For example, you've bought an item for £1,000, so you sell it for £1,200. It doesn't matter that you've seen one on the internet for £10,000. You do that all the time in order to turn stuff over as quickly as possible. It's called 'grocering' because you get your stock and you put a standard margin of say 10 or 15 per cent on it and sell it as fast you can, just like a grocer, who gets their stock in the morning and sells it before it goes off. You put your items in the back of the van and you drive it to a dealer and you make a profit. Not £5 profit or £10 profit if you can possibly avoid it. If you're selling a nice chest of drawers and you can make £100 profit, take it. If they're going to give you £50, take it and do it again. If you can make £50 or £40 profit ten times a day, that's very nice money in your pocket every day. And that's completely achievable. It just takes a bit of hard work, going out sourcing items, putting them in the back of your van and selling them as fast as you can. And once you get into the rhythm of grocering like this, it becomes easy and fun.

You might not want to go that route, of course. Perhaps you have a piece and you're sure you've seen one priced for a fortune. If that is the case, there will be nuances that separate it from all the others. Either that or the dealer doesn't know what they've got and thinks it's way better than it actually is.

That's the point of this book and why I've been so determined to write it. The better the people in this business are, the better and more honest the business will be. We want people to know what they're doing. We want them to take the time to really understand their market. So, ignore what you've seen. Concentrate on making your profit. You've bought the item for £1,000 and you want to sell it for £1,200 and get that 20 per cent mark-up. If you think you can get £1,500 out of it, fine, but £1,200 is decent. Working on that kind of margin you'll be selling into the trade and that's where you need to establish your reputation. Trade business is the best business.

Now this is the difficult bit: you don't want to undersell but you shouldn't try and oversell either. This is where you can get it wrong, even if you are dealing with something very straightforward. You obviously don't want to undersell an item and wipe out your profit but you also need to allow the person who's buying it to make a profit as well. If you reckon that an item is worth £1,000 and you've paid £400, you need to ask for £500 or £600, so the buyer sees there's potentially another £400 or £500 to be made and they will buy it. You've got that balance just about right. They're really happy because they're making money, and you're making a decent amount of money as well. That's where you want to be. That's the sweet spot. There should be a little bit of pain on both sides. You feel like you're just slightly underselling it and they feel like they're just overpaying, and when you get those two things rubbing together, that's when the price is right. READ THAT AGAIN!

To reiterate, if you've got something really good, if you've done your homework and you know everything about it, if you've bought it for £1,000 and you really believe it's worth £10,000, you're not going to get that if you're a new dealer. My advice would be to take the item to the very best dealer in your chosen field, the top person who will get the top money because they've established their reputation and have the right market presence. Show them the piece. Ask them if they can give you £4,000. If they're selling it, they're going to put it up for £10,000, though the chances are they're not going to get that. They might get £8,000 and it's going to cost them £1,000 to process. So, at £8,000 they're making £4,000 minus the grand they've spent processing (showroom, staff, advertising, etc.). We're talking about the top dog in their field, remember? The person with all the right contacts acquired over decades. The person with the fabulous showroom and massive stock, all of which costs loads, so you must allow them to make that profit. You're still making yours so don't be greedy. If you go for top money straight away, you're going to piss off all the big dealers. The chances are you won't get top money anyway and that top dog might have the piece for years. They can afford that. You can't. You want to have it for just a few hours before you sell it on. Turn it over. Make your money and be respectful because this is the essence of trading.

Move Your Stock Quickly

Once you have bought your stock, you need to turn it over and get all your money back – plus your profit, and it is helpful to aim to do that in a month, although it doesn't have to be exactly a month – I'm just using that as an example because that's a target I set for myself. If you want to, you can make it a quarter, which also works well in terms of taxes. With my business today, I chart every day, every week, every month and every three months. Then, after three months, I take another look at an item and decide if there is anything else that can be done to get it sold. Do I need to reduce the price? Do I need to take new photographs? Am I going to put it into an auction? It's a complete rethink of what I'm doing, and in my mature business three months is the norm. But one month is a good time period to work towards turning stock over when you're just starting out. Whatever initial timeframe you set for yourself, you are going to need a no-holds-barred work ethic if you're to thrive in this business, so it's also good to have something to aim for. And how that first period pans out will probably set the pattern for how things will be.

If you want to succeed, you need to treat dealing as a business and not as a hobby. And if you set parameters, you'll create a framework for your work that will stand you in good stead for your entire career. Mine is based around hard work, early mornings and late nights. I also set myself goals; for example, my working week is structured around my newsletters, which go out on Wednesdays and Fridays. So, I make sure that every Wednesday and Friday I have fresh stock ready to be photographed and included in the newsletters. In the meantime, I've got four days (Saturday, Sunday, Monday and

Tuesday) to buy more stock, have it restored if necessary, and get it photographed and listed for the Wednesday newsletter. Then I've got Wednesday and Thursday to get organised for the Friday newsletter. And this gives my working a constant rhythm. I'm out finding stock, I'm checking and looking at restoration and photographing stock, I'm writing descriptions, and then I'm selling. It's a business with clear parameters to work to.

For you, that Wednesday and Friday release of stock might be an antiques fair that you do every Saturday morning. So, by every Saturday morning, you have to ensure that you've got fresh stock, cleaned and ready for sale. This means that on a Monday morning, you've got to get out of bed and go and find fresh stock, or talk to your restorers, or do some more research into your pieces, all in preparation for selling at the weekly fair on Saturday. You're running it as a business. Remember, it's the 'antiques business'.

I recently met with a guy who's been in the trade all his life, one of the very best dealers out there. He's 77 years old and he's been doing it since he was 16. He left the house at seven in the morning, jumped in his car and drove miles to drop some stools at my warehouse for me to sell for him on my website. He was also in the process of getting together stock for a fair, and he was selling through me; he was also buying with other dealers in mind. This is what he does all at the same time. He's able to because he has established a structure to work within, and he never deviates from it. His years of experience allow him to have lots of irons in the fire and work with many people simultaneously because he's built up a network like no other and has set the parameters in a way that allows him to keep on top of everything. His success began with the right work ethic. The point I'm making is that the work ethic you establish and the timescales and parameters you work to set the tone for your life as an antiques dealer. The quicker you sell, the more you can buy. It's something I learnt from the very beginning. I put the same pressure on myself now as I did then.

Once you have the stock, prepare it for sale then sell it. (Sounds easy if you say it quickly, doesn't it?) That's how you spend the rest of that month or quarter, and you do it every day. Buying and selling are separate events – so as soon as you buy it, you need to sell it. While you're at the next dealer's, auction or fair, you should be trying to sell what's in the back of your van while you're buying the next items.

The minute I get something I want to sell it. If I'm buying something at an auction, I'll sometimes have someone in mind to sell it to. While I'm waiting for the next lot to come up, I'll send them some pictures of the item I've just bought and quote them a price that includes my percentage, and occasionally the item is sold on without me ever having handled it. If not, the item goes into stock anyway.

Work hard to buy. Work hard to sell. The key to making inroads is moving stock quickly and effectively. If you're out buying your first tranche of stock and you get the opportunity to sell the very first item you bought, sell it. Never hold back. That other dealer I just mentioned is a prime example. In my opinion, he is the yardstick by which the rest of us are measured. Two days before he was due to set up at a major antiques fair, an American dealer came into his warehouse and bought everything he was taking to the fair. Now, he could've said, 'That's for the fair,' but he didn't. He took the sale that was presented to him, because that's the way he's always approached this business. It's the right way – in my opinion, the only way. With everything he planned to sell already sold, he went to the fair with nothing, whizzed round before it opened, bought enough stock from the other dealers to fill his stand, and sold it all again.

Sell it. Get it gone. Move it on. At the beginning in particular, you're not in the position where you can hold on to stock – you haven't got enough knowledge, you haven't got enough experience and you don't have enough contacts. It doesn't matter if you find the most amazing item, the best thing you've ever seen in your life, and every fibre in your being is telling you to keep it, cherish it, hold on to it. Don't do it. Sell it. Leave your emotions out of everything you do when it comes to selling. You can maybe keep certain things later on, but not when you're starting out, and remember, they will all be sold eventually. Buy the item, do the homework you need to identify it properly and photograph it well. Then sell it.

I recently met a guy who was new to the trade. He found himself with a really nice sofa, but instead of selling it on quickly, he slapped a high retail price on it and refused to offer a trade price, as was his prerogative. He'd been lucky enough to be in the right place at the right time and had bought it cheap. He told me he wanted £15,000 and asked me what I thought it was worth (never ask this, as it's just not done in the business). I told him it didn't matter what I thought – it was his opinion that mattered. He asked if I wanted to buy it. Of course I did! But he was asking way too much money – £15,000 is full retail for an experienced dealer who has the kind of contacts who would want to buy it. He kept on hassling me, so I told him I'd give him £5,800. He would still be making a decent profit, but he balked at the fact he was leaving loads in it for me. If I had been in his position, I'd have sold it at the £5,800, thereby establishing a working relationship with a more experienced dealer, one I could revisit. As I've said, this is very important – it's the way to get on. It's the way to make the right contacts. I explained to him that I wouldn't get anywhere near the £15,000 full retail – that was for someone else much further up the line – and the most I would make was £2,000. He didn't accept that, which meant he refused to accept how the business works. He was sure I was ripping him off so I could make the profit he couldn't. That's not how things work. He had completely the wrong attitude. Of course, it's hard to sell for a smaller profit when you know you've found something wonderful. But, again, it's important that you do. Unless you have the right contacts, you're not going to make that top-level money . . . yet.

Trade to Trade

Working with the trade is quick and straightforward, so you want to start selling within the trade as early as you can. The way to do that is to go and meet as many dealers as possible. You've got your stock, the clock is ticking and you have to get going. I get people new to the trade calling me all the time. They'll phone up or sometimes just turn up with a carload and, although I hate doing it, I politely turn most of them away because they haven't got it right. However, on the odd occasion, they've got something I potentially want and I buy it.

Show up with your stock having researched that dealer first so you know you're at least in the right ballpark. Make sure you've priced well, giving yourself the wriggle room you're going to need for trade discount. Pick a dealer you think might genuinely buy the items you've bought and don't be a smart arse. Don't tell them you've been doing it for years – tell them the truth, because they will see right through you. Tell them you've just started out and you've got a few things in the back of the van you're wondering if they'd be kind enough to have a look at.

You can lower your margin a little bit if you absolutely have to, but you still need to make a profit. You need that profit, but a big part of the business is about making connections and when you start out that's even more important. The first person you go and see might have no interest in what you've got right now but they might next time. What's

SELLING

important is the connection and the fact you've presented yourself professionally, so that they take you seriously. You might not sell anything to the first ten dealers, you might not hit it off with even half, maybe there are only three who want to talk to you, but hopefully there will be one with whom you really make a connection. That's somebody you can always deal with, but they have to be the right person in the first place. There's no point showing up with a vanload of chairs if all the dealer sells is stamps. Make sure you're in the same realm and make that connection. Make enough connections and you have a business. If that's as far as you want to go, you can make a living within that network. You can pick people you admire, people you aspire to emulate; alternatively, you can pick someone who's local who you think is all right and try and work with them. Remember, the business is the same no matter how long you've been trading. We all need stock and we need it all the time, so there will always be another dealer out there wanting to talk to you.

I have a very good friend in the trade who turned up at my door about 15 years ago in an old 4x4. In the back he had a pair of lamps and some other bits and bobs and did exactly what I'm proposing you do. He told me he'd just got started and had finished a house clearance up the road and asked if I'd come and have a look. Sure, why not? He was genuine, honest; he told me how it was so I was more than happy to see what he had. As it turned out I bought two country house pillar lamps and a Chinese vase lamp, and they were among the best examples I've ever had. Fifteen years later we're good friends and I still buy from him. I trust him. He's always done the right thing. If I don't want to buy something, he's all right about it. If I do want something, I make that decision quickly and pay him immediately. Both payment to you and from you is really important. Don't give credit. Don't ask for it. Do not let anyone walk away without at least giving them an invoice. Make sure the money side of things is done thoroughly and quickly. Make sure it's absolutely clear who's paying who for what and in what condition. Do not leave grey areas, because they cause problems.

Selling dealer to dealer is the single hardest thing to do in the antiques business but, in my opinion, it's also the best way of working, because you are dealing with people who are knowledgeable and are less likely to mess you about. You can be 100 per cent honest and say, 'It's a great chair, but the arm's falling off or the leg's a bit loose. It's this much. You can take it away.' It should be that straightforward. It can be really tough though, especially at the beginning, because you have to get to know everybody. You have to be the most hard-working person on the planet. One of my very, very good friends is a trade-only dealer. If he absolutely has to, he will sell the occasional item to the public, but he doesn't really want to, as it's often more hassle than it's worth.

An exclusively trade-to-trade dealer is not something you become overnight – it takes at least 20 or 30 years. The top trade people are the most intelligent, the hardest working and, most of the time, they're participating in the greatest deals going on. These are deals no one else knows about. They don't tell anybody what they're doing, they don't advertise what they're doing and only those who need to know are involved. If you're lucky enough to meet one of these guys and start an association with them where you can buy from them or even sell to them then you are blessed.

When you're dealing with another dealer, they make the decisions right there and they should pay you very quickly. You're making a profit and you're making a friend and that's the most important thing to remember. Now, because it's trade, I can hear you asking if you have to compromise on your profit margin. You shouldn't have to, no, because this business only works if everyone is making money. When it comes to the trade, I suggest you add 20 per cent to the price you paid, then the costs, tax, marketing, etc., then add another 20 per cent on top of it to create the 'dealing' room you might need to ultimately make your 20 per cent margin. There is usually a little back and forth, but as long as you're making a clear profit after costs and tax, be happy to sell it and move on. Do it again and again and again. Keep doing it and you'll make a living in the antiques business.

There's one trade-to-trade guy I deal with all the time. He spends up to £50,000 a month with me and he's probably making between £5,000 and £10,000 on that. I'm not the only dealer he's talking to. The really good guys have at least eight or ten people like me they sell to. Add that up and they're making hundreds of thousands of pounds a month selling antiques to other dealers. But don't think you'll be doing that anytime soon. They're trade dealers not runners and it's important not to confuse the two.

Runners, as we call them, also work trade to trade. When you get a bit of experience, say two to five years in, you'll have enough knowledge and a large enough network of dealers to 'run' items between them. You've got your £2,000 van, your

SELLING

£5,000 worth of stuff in the back and you run between the various dealers in your area. You make your money and go off again to buy more stock and run that around to them as well. That's how it works, the really basic stuff; a bit of 'grocering' combined with a bit of 'running'.

The two best trade dealers in this country only deal with really good stuff though, and sell upwards into the trade. One's got 50 years' experience, the other's got 40 and all they do is sell to the trade, leaving a very large margin for the dealers at the top of the food chain. That's how they've survived and flourished. As far as I'm concerned it's what makes them the best of the best. If you can do that when everyone knows you're just starting out then you'll instantly command respect. You'll demonstrate to those top dealers that you understand how this business works and when you bring them the next piece they will give you the time of day. That dealer will want to deal with you again and again, and, if you want, you can have a whole business based on just a handful of people.

So, you've paid £1,000, we've established you need to make 20 per cent and I've mentioned the wriggle room you're going to need when trading dealer to dealer. Do that with all your stock and ignore what other people are selling similar items for on their websites. You know what you paid for each item – that's what's important – and you want to move it on quickly, so put a margin on it and sell it. If you sell quickly (which is the point), you'll probably think you could have got more – don't think that. There will be a time for getting more; right now is the time to be learning. What you're doing is buying your education. There's never been a truer word said about this business – you literally buy your education. The whole idea is to buy and sell as many things as you can as quickly as you can; your knowledge will grow with each transaction. Equally, if you make a mistake, you will learn just as quickly.

Appro

'Appro' is short for 'approval', and it is an important facet of selling within the trade, with strict rules that need to be applied right from the off.

From time to time an interior designer might spot an item you have listed, phone up and ask you to put it on 'reserve', but this is different from appro. They're probably working on a project and what you're offering might fit that project but it might not. When you're established in the trade you can if you want reserve an item for someone, but right now you just want to turn it over as quickly as possible. If something is on hold, you're not making any money – it's not fluid. You can't afford that. Not now. If you agree to it, they might come back to you today but it might be tomorrow or the day after that or the day after that, and that's no good to you. So, be very honest with them and say, 'Look, I've only got a small margin in that item' – meaning you're already at your best price and there's no room for negotiation – 'I can reserve it for an hour but that's all. I'd love to help more but I can't.' An hour will be no good to them, but you made the gesture without compromising your own position. And they will (or should) respect that.

Appro is when you get a call from a prospective client or decorator and they ask you to bring an item for them to have a look at in situ in their house or property. Before you agree to do that, a number of things have to be sorted. First, you should agree a price in advance. If they've got it in their house, and you turn around and say, 'Well, it's five grand,' and they say, 'What are you talking about? I thought it was three,' you're wasting each other's time. Second, if it's a long way and there are costs involved, you have to agree that they will cover them. Third, make sure you tell them that you will be taking the item away that day if possible. That really helps with the sale – it concentrates their mind on buying. Fourth, if they do want it, agree that payment will be made as soon as possible – whatever the timescale, just make sure it's agreed before you go. Set your stall out properly. It's easier, it's honest and it's less hassle all round.

If you're not taking it yourself and need to send a carrier (which we do a lot), the carrier will usually put the piece into the house (what we call 'placed') if it's arranged prior. That takes time and effort. They may need to take another person with them depending on the size of the item, and you have to make sure the client agrees beforehand to cover that cost. If they don't want it, it goes back on the van to be returned and they pay the carrier's costs. That can be direct or to you – either way, it's imperative you agree in advance. If they're not willing to take the risk then neither should you. At this stage you're setting the ground rules you're going to play by and you have to protect that all important margin.

One of the great things about appro is that once you have an item in someone's house, it creates a connection that makes it more likely they'll buy it. It's the same reason that car salespeople get you to sit in a car when you go to a showroom – it's easier to imagine yourself driving the car once you're behind the wheel, and it is easier to make the leap and buy an antique once it's in their house than when it is sitting in a showroom or shop. Last year, I took a significant number of valuable items to a client's house on appro. My team and I spent two days putting the items in and dressing the house for them. When the client walked in, they loved it and bought the lot. But they needed to see it in place – there's no way they would have bought all of those items just by looking at my website.

Running Your Own Shop

I discovered a long time ago that the secret to a successful shop is to create an environment that people want to come to. This is their time off. They've probably worked really hard all week and are thinking, *Let's go and buy something fun. Let's go and have some lunch. Let's make a day of it.* They come to an antiques shop because they want to be surprised. They want to be engaged. They want to find something interesting that they can take home with them. And if they've had a good experience, they'll tell their friends about it, and they'll come back.

An antiques shop can therefore be very rewarding and make you money if you do it right, but it is not just there so you can sell things. Unlike any other retail environment I can think of, an antiques shop is also a tool to help you to build your business. People will walk in and sell you things. You will get house calls. You'll get leads. You'll get private sellers coming in and you'll get trade sellers. That's where the money is made – in the buy, remember? If you check out some antiques shops, you'll soon identify the people who really know what they're doing. They're the ones with signs outside that indicate they buy. Nothing pulls people in like a sign saying WE BUY. Everybody's got something to sell and everybody wants money. That's how you make cash out of a shop. My shop was set up as a fairy high-end antiques retailer, but I still had loads of people walking in with good stuff – and I mean really good things – that they wanted to sell. They saw what I was selling and thought, *I've got some of that*. It's all about attracting buyers and sellers.

That said, I would advise against a shop in the early days of your career. At the beginning, it makes more sense to concentrate on the basic principles and learn how to deal with the trade. There's no point in opening a shop when you haven't learnt to deal with the people you need to be dealing with. I've already said that dealing with the trade is the best kind of business. If you don't know how to do that and you've opened a shop, you're spending money on a fixed asset and not making the most of it.

If you do acquire a retail outlet at some point, you have to prepare the pieces you buy for selling in that environment. It's very different from selling at a fair because the space you have must be used to create the best possible ambience. We call them shops, but really an antiques shop is a showroom. You're showing off your stock, so the lighting has to be right, the feel, the atmosphere. As far as the items themselves are concerned, the same basic principles apply. Make sure they're clean. Make sure they're visible. If it's a chair or a campaign chest, make sure it doesn't have 20 books on top of it or half a dozen lamps or something. Make sure nothing is in the way of it being displayed in the most sympathetic way it can be. And make sure the price is on it – if something isn't priced it's a hurdle, because most people won't ask the prince for fear of embarrassment and you can't sell it.

It's also really important to make sure it's clearly labelled. It doesn't have to say 'Fantastic, wonderful, amazing'. Just state what it is and be able to tell the prospective buyer whether it's had any restoration. This is what you don't say: 'A wonderful, amazing [one I really love] chest of drawers in a really good colour. It's got nice big drawers for putting all your socks in – £500.' Don't put something on the label like 'old' or 'vintage'. Neither really tells you very much. Do you want to know the biggest crime in my book? 'Victorian.' How often have you been into an antiques shop, emporium or a fair somewhere and seen the word 'Victorian'? If I see 'Victorian' on something I just think, *You lazy sod*. At least give it a decade – the Victorian era spanned nearly eight decades. Do the research, look it up. You'll find most of what you need on the internet. Specify. Put 1860s or 1890s. Do not just write 'Victorian'. Put English. Put Welsh. Put Irish, French, Italian, whatever it may be. Trust me, all of these things will help you sell it.

The right label would be something like '1870s French. Original paint – £500'. Simple, effective and to the point. It tells the buyer exactly what they need to know and that makes the item more attractive. They'll check it out and if it's too much they'll walk away. If it's not, then: 'Wow! Look at that. I love it.' Whether you think it's the best one or whatever, keep your opinion about any piece you're selling in your head – do not write it on the label. If they ask you can tell them what you think but otherwise your opinion is irrelevant. 'A wonderful fluffy this that and the other.' Don't do it.

Another simple and apparently obvious detail – make sure your shop is clean. The number of shops or showrooms I go to that are dirty, have rubbish strewn around, one thing stacked on top of the other – it beggars belief. Cups, empty crisp packets, overflowing bins. Just because there are no hard and fast rules in what we do doesn't mean we can get away with anything. Some people don't care and others think that their place looking like a junkyard is funny. They think a great clutter of odds and ends dotted all over the place with no planning, no symmetry to the display, is a good thing. It's not. Trust me.

As I said, make your shop a really attractive place to be. Remember, it's got your name above the door. It's a reflection of you. So, think about that: take time to consider what you want people to think about you and make it a little haven. When they come through the door they've stepped into the world you've created and you want them to enjoy the experience. You want them to feel comfortable and you want to slow them down. I believe there's an art to laying out a shop, particularly in the antiques business. There are ways you can slow your customers down so they spend longer, enjoy more and are more likely to buy. In good retail environments, you can't walk in a straight line, because you walk faster in a straight line and are less likely to stop and look around. Why do you think it is such a pain to get through the duty-free shops in airports? Because the layouts slow you down and you're more likely to browse. You can do the same in an antiques shop. Lay out your stock in interesting ways that makes people want to delve deeper, around the back of the display case and down the alleyway and then up the stairs. You want them to come in and say, 'It's nice in here. I'm going to have a good look around.' If you have a big pile of stuff on one side of the shop and a big pile of stuff on the other with an aisle down the middle, they'll walk down the aisle, turn around and walk straight back out again. You are not selling fruit and veg; you're selling things that need to be imbued with a little bit of excitement.

I once asked the guy who runs what I think is the best shop in the UK what the secret to his success was, and he said to me, 'You know what? I make people think they've found something.' He's not trying to trick anyone. He's just knows that what's exciting about going to an antiques shop is finding something you love that you think no one else would have spotted.

So let your customer think. Let them wander. Buying something from you is not a necessity – it's not like going out to pick up some groceries.

SELLING

Remember, we sell things they don't need but want. This is an experience, something they should be enjoying. The money they spend is going to make their home or garden a more aesthetically pleasing place to be and they've worked very hard to get that money. It's part of a process, a lifetime's journey. Think about all that's led up to the moment they walk into your shop to buy an antique that has no purpose other than giving them pleasure. Now they have the home they've always dreamed of, they want to enjoy it by buying just the right items to go in it. Entering your shop, your showroom, your world, is part and parcel of the journey they've been on, so make sure it's as enjoyable as possible.

You're in sales now, and the best sales people never appear to be selling. It's effortless. They're artists – what they do is guide, facilitate and direct. If you're selling antiques, you're there to shift stock, but that has to be done with care and a level of expertise and finesse, part and parcel of the preparation that ensures a visit to your shop is an immersive experience. Never forget, selling antiques is what you do every day. Not them. They might never have bought an antique. Stepping through the door of your shop might be a totally new experience and you need to make sure it's truly memorable. In 30 years' time when they're sat there with their grandchildren running round you want them to say: 'I'm going to give that chest of drawers to Dicky. You know the one I mean? Remember the day we bought it? We were in Stow-on-the-Wold in that wonderful shop and bought it from that lovely couple? D'you remember? We only paid about three hundred quid. It's worth at least two grand now. What about that for an investment. Let's give it to little Dicky.'

That's the kind of memory the right ambiance, the right display, the right labelling can instil. How your shop is laid out matters. It's all part of what you're trying to do – you're trying to create something permanent. Everything you sell has had a life you know little about – every chair, every lamp, every piece of nineteenth-century furniture. By definition, an antique creates continuity and a connection with the past, and I believe every antiques shop should be part of that sense of permanence. It should be part of the texture of every town, like the corner shop or butchers, a place you can always rely on, a world apart you can always visit. It should always be there. It used to be like that. It wasn't long ago when every town had an antiques shop, maybe more than one, but they don't any more. They're so much harder to maintain nowadays, what with high commercial rents

SELLING

and soaring costs, not to mention the competition from online retailing. But if you absolutely must have one, make it the best you can. Make sure your customers can rely on you to be there with new and innovative stock they can own and cherish. And make sure you're open when you say you're going to be. Whatever it says on the door, on your website, your Instagram, you can't dick people around. If you say you're going to be open between 9am and 5pm, you have to be. There's nothing worse for a customer than not knowing when a shop will be open, especially if they've travelled from far away to get to you. If it's hit and miss or suck it and see, if it's half-arsed, so will you be.

Before you embark on the retail road, remember that a shop can be – in fact, usually is – a very expensive, gilded anchor, weighing you down. You probably need to be open seven days a week and it takes a huge amount of time and effort. Over the years I've had a lot of different shops, including the whole fourth floor at Liberty in London. I've had big antiques fair units. I've had five different retail outlets, two of them massive. It's a lot of work and it's all-consuming. If you don't manage it right it can stop you going out and buying. You can't sell if you don't buy, which means you're going to have to employ somebody to do the selling for you. You have to make sure they're the right person. That might sound obvious, but this is a unique business in which no two items are exactly the same and no matter who you employ or how much you pay them, they're never going to have the level of commitment that you do. So, be careful because it's your name above the door and your reputation is at stake every day.

We touched on it just now but I'll reiterate: you're actually selling yourself. You are your business so the same rules apply to selling as buying. Make sure whoever is doing the selling – whether it's you or someone else – is smart, presentable, polite and honest. One of the most basic requirements is personal hygiene. We've all been in the shop where the pervading odour is sweat – old, dried BO. It happens a lot in this business where not every shop is laid out as well as it could be, where stock is piled ceiling high and it took a lot of sweat to get it up there. People notice. They judge you (they do – deal with it). Make the best impression and give yourself the best shot. There was a time when you could get away with a sweat-stained T-shirt with half your dinner spilled down the front but you can't any more. If the owner of the piece you're buying is a slovenly old slob, then generally that will be reflected in the piece you're buying. First impressions are everything. You only see someone or something for the first time once and people have bought into you and what you're doing within the first few seconds of walking through the door. So, if you don't open on time or the place is smelly, if you can't see anything properly, if the pricing is missing, and the lighting or heating are incorrect, you're not going to make as much money as you could.

The better salesperson you can find, the more stock you're going to shift, so don't stint. Go the extra mile to make sure they're perfect to represent you. I had my friend David working for me in the shop in Conwy – a better salesman you will not find. Watching him was like seeing an artist at work. I could watch him all day, the ease with which he guided the sale from the moment someone walked in the door right through to the inevitable conclusion. He would hold their hand all the way and usually they would leave with more than just the item they first wanted to purchase. David would have them coming back again and again. He would sell an item and send another out on appro that might complement it. He'd say something like: 'Well, you've bought that, so let's get it home and let's take that pair of chairs with it. I'll come along as well. You don't have to pay for them – let's just see what they look like.' He was attentive, polite. He didn't talk about himself; he talked about them. Being a salesperson is like going on a first date. If you've got any sense, you don't talk about yourself, you talk about the person you're with.

'God, you look fantastic. I love your hair like that. It really suits you.'

Make it all about them. That's what a good salesperson does and they're worth their weight in gold. If you don't want to employ anyone you don't have to – you can be that salesperson. Either way you need to get the basics right and put on some deodorant. Brush your hair. I know, I know, it sounds obvious, but I come across people all the time who don't do the basics properly. If you want to make money, if you want to come across as a pro, then be professional. This is not just some piddly arsed thing on the side – this is your job. This is your career. This is your money. Treat it with some respect. Treat the people who come through your door with the same respect. Do it properly.

Just now we talked about the layout of your shop, the ambiance and how, ideally, it should be a place where you slow people down so they really enjoy the experience. I believe in every retail outlet there's one room or area of floor space where selling is most effective. A sweet spot. We call it 'The Money Room'. I'll guarantee there will be one section of your shop where things sell really well. It can be down to the atmosphere, the feel, the light, the layout, whatever. Make sure you find it. You will. It'll be there. Work out where it is and exploit it.

When I was a kid, I used to buy and sell cars. I was doing it at 15. It was ridiculous really but I loved it. By the time I was about 18 I was making really good money. Officially I was on the YTS, getting £17.50 a week, but I was making £300 or £400 at the weekend buying and selling cars. I used to sell out of the back yard at my parents' house in Glan Conwy. They had this lovely willow tree, a really big picturesque one. It was the first thing you saw as you came down the drive so I used to park the car I was selling at a slight angle underneath the tree with the wheels turning outwards to make it look like it was leaving. When a buyer turned up, that's what they saw first: the car they were thinking of buying, all shined up, looking as if it was already leaving. I tell you what, it sold them. That spot, that way of displaying the car, a sweet spot, it sold them time after time after time. If I parked them facing backwards it didn't work. If I parked them sideways it didn't work.

It had to be facing the front with the wheels at an angle as if there were someone at the wheel and the car was leaving. It never failed, and it stuck with me.

You use every advantage you can find because buying and selling might sound easy, but it isn't. For some people it might come naturally. It did with me, thank god. I'd begun buying and selling early, so I had a head start. I'm rubbish at most things but I'm good at buying and selling. I always have been. I was swapping and selling Doc Martens, bikes and air rifles at the age of 11. If it doesn't come so naturally to you it doesn't matter. That's why I'm writing this book, to offer as much help as I can. I know in some places it might sound like I'm having a rant, but that's only because I care so much about the business. I want it to be the best it can be and, if you're going to get involved, I want you to be the best you can be. If we all take that attitude, the business will continue to grow. We'll all go the extra mile and the result will be of benefit to everyone.

So, when it comes to retail look for the sweet spot in your premises and use it to the full advantage. Play with it. Have fun. This is your baby. The antiques trade is a business where you can do pretty much whatever you want, so experiment – be artistic. A shop is an opportunity to make your mark, create

SELLING

your own aesthetic, and that's what the best dealers do. Make sure your horizons are as broad as they can be, use your imagination and don't allow yourself to be constrained.

It's a 24-7 Business

You need to be available on the phone from the minute you wake up to the minute you go to sleep, seven days a week. You have to remember you're selling something that people don't generally need – it's something they want, so you've got to be available when it's their downtime, and that applies to the trade as much as it does to retail.

If you get into the retail side of the business in a big way, you'll start to climb the income ladder in terms of your clients and come to realise that this is their fun time. This is what they've worked for – fun money. It sounds ridiculous, but very rich people have fun money. I have a client who makes £3 million a year – a million goes to his wife, a million goes into savings and a million is his fun money. That's a true story. I deal with him all the time and he made no bones about telling me. With someone like that you have to be available to make whatever they want happen as soon as possible. It doesn't matter if it's 11.30 on a Saturday night or 6am on a Sunday, you need to be on the end of the phone.

If you don't want to do that, if you want to turn your phone off, that's fine. I'm just trying to tell you what I did and still do and will continue to do because I believe it's the best way to run my business. Not everyone's the same but I think it's the way to advance most quickly. The more money you can earn, the more things you can buy, which means the more you have to sell, the more people you will meet, etc. The ball never stops rolling. It goes on and on and on and it's pretty much all-consuming. There's little room for anything else, including holidays. After I'd been doing it for two decades, I decided to have my first one. I'm not joking. For the first 20 years in this business, I didn't have a single holiday.

Selling Online

A large part of dealing today is done online, where image is everything. The online market is huge. It's massive. You can live solely online without ever having to come down to earth at all if you don't want to, although I would recommend a more diversified approach. And you can buy and sell around the world and not actually meet anybody face to face. The ability to sell globally is the best thing that ever happened to this business. If you pay attention and work it right, it can be phenomenal. I saw the potential immediately and went online in 1999.

To that end, a good website is essential. Make it as concise as possible. It doesn't have to be 50 pages long. It can be as simple as your name and your contact details front and centre, then a list of your stock by category: lighting, seating, cabinetry, statuary, paintings, etc.

No. 1 – Photography

Make sure your photography is good, although you definitely don't need to pay a professional photographer. I've lost count of the times people tell me they can't use a camera. 'I'm rubbish. I don't know which end is up. I don't know anything about lighting. I don't know about setting something up so it looks good.' These days taking a photo couldn't be easier, so stop moaning and learn. Back when I started it was an Instamatic or Polaroid; now the camera on your phone is better than most cameras were back then. So, please, let's not hear any, 'I can't do that. I don't know anything about technology. I can't take a decent picture.' Learn how to take a photograph and get better at it. Be the person who says I can't take decent photographs yet, but I will. I'm going to learn because it's an important part of what I'm doing. Bit of a rant, I know, but it's one of my pet hates. It's putting obstacles in the way of getting where you want to be that just don't need to be there.

Think about what you're doing. The right image of a piece is as important as the piece itself, so apply the same level of care that you did when it came to buying it. If you do use your phone, make sure it's mounted on a tripod, and make sure the picture is scaled correctly so the right height, width and depth is visible. Don't take pictures from above with the lens pointing down because that tells you nothing. Take multiple photographs of details. Take photographs that display what's wrong with an item and make sure the lighting is good. If you try to hide something, I promise it will come back to bite you. Clear the background so you've got a nice easy image to deal with. You need to get this right because people tend to make a subconscious decision about whether or not they'll buy something within the first ten seconds of seeing it. This is your easiest way of selling something. Give your potential client a good strong image.

No. 2 – Detail

List the measurements and make sure you include the dimensions in centimetres as well as feet and inches. Your customer might be in America, where they use feet and inches, or in Europe where they are metric. Don't make it hard for them. Cover all the bases.

No. 3 – Clarity

As with shop labelling, make sure your description is short, to the point and accurate. The basics are simple:

- What's it made out of?
- Who made it (if you know)?
- What condition is it in?
- What country did it come from?
- What year, or decade or period was it made?

Those are the five basic tenets. You don't need anything more than that. Just the facts. Museum or auction catalogues are a great reference point when it comes to learning about description and labelling.

Once that's set in stone, make sure your website is easily found. Use a snappy, easily remembered name – avoid anything long-winded like Dolly's Emporium of

Delight – and add the address to all aspects of your online presence, especially social media, as I find that more people come to my site that way than via a search engine these days. One of my very good friends described a website as a message in a bottle. You've got the best bottle you've ever seen and the message inside is a work of genius, but people have to be able to find it, so make sure it's visible. Think of it in those terms and you won't go wrong. Also, make sure you have a mailing list sign-up form on the site so people can leave their details. Keeping a client is a lot easier than getting a new one, so ensure you build up your list.

Packing and Shipping

Another important part of selling is making sure that when your client receives the item they've bought it isn't smashed or broken. This means that packing and shipping are essential parts of the job and have to be done right. Get it wrong and you'll have very unhappy customers on the phone wanting their money back. These days the majority of people buy online and you never meet them. That doesn't matter – they're your customers and they want their goods to arrive quickly and in good condition.

If something needs to be shipped – a large item in your showroom, for example – and you can arrange it, then do so. It helps the customer so it helps with the sale and makes the whole transaction go more smoothly. Remember, you do this all the time. They don't. You're the one used to getting stuff packed up and shipped so make sure it's done properly.

No. 1 – Protecting items

Be certain the item is going to get there without being broken. You wouldn't believe the amount of stuff I've seen that's badly packed. I've literally had people post ceramics to me wrapped in paper. It doesn't arrive; nothing is left. All that remains are a few broken bits and pieces. You can't wrap ceramics or glass, anything breakable, in paper. Obvious, right? You'd be amazed. Get yourself geared up. Buy decent boxes and get hold of some recyclable chips or something similar to pack them out. We always use recyclable chips; everything involved in our shipping is recyclable. It makes sense; that's the world we live in. That said, there's nothing wrong with using bubble wrap, old blankets, whatever – it's up to you, just so long as what you're shipping arrives undamaged.

We ship all our furniture in those grey shipping blankets you see us use on TV. We call them donkey blankets; everything is wrapped, taped up then put in boxes that we fill with the recyclable pellets. After the item is secure, we pass it to our carriers. We use two: Chris and Kev. One of them picks stuff up on a daily basis and the other weekly. Once it's left the premises, the carrier takes over completely. When you use the right ones, you have peace of mind. The client is paying for their expertise and you know the item is going to arrive safely.

No. 2 – Dispatch time

When something is paid for, when the money is in your account, make sure the customer receives it as soon as you can get it to them. The quicker the better. It's all part of who you are as a dealer. If something takes for ever, they'll remember. If it's there fast, they will also remember and are much more likely to keep tabs on your shop or website and return as a customer. Don't make them hang on. In general people are impatient. No sooner has money changed hands than the clock starts ticking. A minute in your mind could be an hour in the customer's – a day is a week, a week is a month.

They just want it as fast as you can get it to them, so go the extra mile to make sure they're going to get it as fast as possible. It's very hard to get a new customer but it's easier to keep an old one if you do everything right and equally as easy to lose them if you don't. Above all, be honest about the amount of time something is going to take – honesty's the maxim that runs through every aspect of the trade, including the cost of shipping and how long an item might take to get somewhere. Put it in an email so they know. Don't just forget about it. Don't ever put deliveries on the back burner. People expect to get what they've bought from you quickly.

No. 3 – International shipping

If you're shipping something internationally, do your homework. Like everything else in this trade, it's all about due diligence and preparation. Ask other dealers to help point you in the right direction. For example, if you've got a chair you need to send to California and the client wants it by a certain time, find out what that's going to cost and make sure it's part of the deal. By boat in a group container is the cheapest way of shipping. Air freight is the most expensive. Some people will pay for air freight but not many. Use a good shipper, someone you've heard of, someone reputable – ask about. You've got to transport the item from your warehouse/shop to the shipping agent, but they will handle the rest. If you want to arrange international shipping without an agent, good luck. I would suggest you don't. Leave it to somebody who ships thousands of items a week – let them take care of it. It's a vital part of your business and you can't afford to get it wrong. They know what they're doing so use them.

I once got a call from a guy in Canada. He told me he'd seen a piece of stained glass on the website that he really liked and wanted to come and have a look at. We spoke on the phone and he said: 'I'm in the UK next week. I'll be arriving at Manchester at eleven o'clock on Friday morning so I can be with you at around half twelve.'

'Fine,' I said. 'I'll look forward to seeing you.'

I kept the piece back for him, and had it cleaned and displayed for him. Friday came around, and he turned up at the warehouse, looked at the piece of stained glass and liked it even more once he'd seen it in person.

'OK,' he said. 'I'd like to buy it.'

We did the deal and I asked him if he wanted me to sort out shipping.

'No, that's all right. Just pack it in some bubble wrap and I'll take it with me.'

I thought about that for a moment. 'They're not going to allow you to take it in the cabin on the plane as hand luggage, you know, and if it's in the hold it's bound to get broken.'

'Don't worry,' he said. 'It's my plane.'

You don't get many like that, though there are one or two – that's the beauty of this incredible business. No two days are the same, no two people. Nevertheless, my advice would be to always use shipping agents – unless they have their own plane, of course. Build the shipping costs into the deal. It's over and above the price of the item and should be at cost – there's no need for you to make money on shipping. Sometimes, to get a sale away, we might offer to cover half the cost for the client. We'll look at the international shipping rates and, if we've got a bit of profit in the item and can soak a bit up, we'll do it. It works better and you've enhanced your relationship with them.

No. 4 – Keeping a record

Before we ship an item, we take a short video or lots of photographs. I'd suggest you do the same, because you'll have a record of the date from the video or photos, and you'll have a record of the condition the item was in when it left your warehouse, so if there is any damage, you can prove it happened after it was shipped. You want to avoid damage, though, so go to town on your wrapping.

As I said, this is a really boring topic, but if you're going to learn how to be an antiques dealer, it's an integral part of the business, now more so than ever. You have to get it right or it's going to cost you a load of money. I don't need to say any more – most of it is common sense and all you need to do is apply it.

Restocking

You've spent £5,000 on what you consider to be the best you can buy and now you're turning the stock over. If you've got £7,000 in your bank account at the end of that first month, or whatever timeframe you've set yourself, you've done dead right. That's the essence of this business. It's how it should be, but this is where it gets hard because now you need to buy more stock. This is the balance, this is the thing that's really, really difficult. No matter how experienced you are, it's really tough. Even I find it hard after all the years. These days I'm dealing with large quantities of stock coming in and

SELLING

out every day. It takes time to get to that stage, but it's the art of the business. Any business.

I do the same things today I've always done and you should too. That means doing your research, making sure you're still buying the right stuff and not panicking, and keeping tabs on your margins. You're not doing this for free – the margins have to be there. It's vital that you don't just stand there throwing money at stuff. You do have to gamble but you've got to keep a working capital. I tended to plough all my money back into the business when I was starting out – I still do to an extent – but you also need to be savvy and not put yourself in financial difficulty. Beyond that, you can never have enough stock. I always think you're better off having your money in stock because it means you've got options. So, the minute you start to sell your initial stock, you have to go out and find more. Get in the car and visit other dealers. Go to antiques fairs and take part in online auctions. The search never ends. I get up on a Saturday morning and by eight or nine o'clock I'm somewhere in the country waiting for a shop to open so I can buy more stock. Remember, this is the fun bit. This is what you've dreamt of. And it's where your money's made too – your money is made in the buy. I can't tell you that enough.

Some dealers pour everything into selling their initial stock, meaning they have a good first month, but if they don't think about restocking at the same time, it goes quickly downhill after that. People in this situation might take a month or two to get another good bunch of stuff together and then they have another decent period. Their businesses are characterised by peaks and troughs. That's no good. You want things to be smooth all the way through. Don't buy then sell – buy and sell at the same time. This means you're constantly restocking. It's not easy, but you've got to keep your foot down all the time.

It's about working hard but also working smart. If you work hard, keep your head and don't just throw money at stuff, you'll have great stock all the time. If you're a bit lazy and go to your next-door neighbour and buy a cast-iron fish out of their garden, you're not going to make any money. You need to take a measured approach. Look at the right piece and decide if you can sell it quickly, which will allow you to move on to the next one. Where people go wrong is when they take the scatter-gun approach and end up with £5,000 of stock that nobody wants. That's when they get disheartened. They've spent all their money. They're looking at all these items and they go:

SELLING

'Bugger, I've got no money and nobody wants to buy my stuff.'

It's happened to us all at one time or another, so when it happens to you, which it undoubtedly will, shove the dead stock in the back of your car, drive to another dealer and try to sell it. If that doesn't work, go to an antiques fair or an antiques centre and talk to the people there. Put more adverts up. Put it on Instagram, email people and ask if they'd be interested. If the price is attractive, you will sell it. Sometimes, though, you might have to sell for what you paid for it, or you might have to take even less. If you're going to take a loss, take it quickly.

Taking a Loss and Cashflow

Everybody in the antiques trade takes a loss now and again, apart from a dealer friend of mine in Scotland who pointedly refuses. If she thinks she's going to take a hit, she won't sell the item and just hangs on to it. It works for her, but I don't work like that. Sometimes I have to take a loss and when I do, I generally take it fairly quickly. I'll bite the bullet and sell it for what I bought it for or less in order to get some money back in and moving. If I've got £1,000 in something and I've got it wrong, that's £1,000 I'm out and I'm not going to get it back. It's a grand sitting on the shelf that I can't get to. If, on the other hand, I sell it quickly for £700, then the loss is only £300 and I can use the £700 to try and get that £300 back. Crazy, I know.

If you don't want to do that you can take another approach: 'I'll wait then. If it ain't worth a grand today I'll sit on it and wait till it's worth £1,200.' I'd rather have some money back so I can keep turning it over. Sometimes I'll pay too much money for something but won't take a loss because I know I'm going to keep it long term or with a future auction sale in mind. That's another subject altogether, the long-term buy as an investment. I do quite a lot of that – too much, in fact, but we'll discuss it in more detail later.

For now, you're taking a loss. Everybody has to suck it up at some point. But keep the money turning over, because money is the tool of your trade. It's your hammer, your spanner. You can't fix a car if you haven't got any spanners and you can't buy and sell antiques if you don't have any money. So, if you're going to take a loss, take it quickly and move on. Blow it out. That's an old saying in the trade. 'I've just blown it out.' Blowing it out is getting close to your money back, which is a nice way of saying 'I've made a loss.' The other saying is 'I've just pushed it.' A push is an Americanism that means you've sold it for what you paid for it. You've just pushed it. You haven't done anything with it, you've just pushed it. That's OK too. If you really have to, if it's going to cause you problems, get out of it because it'll only depress you to keep looking at your thousand quid all tied up. It's a hard lesson but one that has to be learnt. If you lose money, I guarantee you'll learn very quickly – remember, you're buying your education.

You're not going to get it right all the time. Sometimes you have to take a hit in order to keep that money moving. I recently took a £300 hit on a cupboard. I bought it for £5,800 and had to sell for £5,500. A guy was in the shop, and he wanted to buy it. I'd had it for a month – it was sitting there doing nothing. He offered £5,500 and I took the decision to get that money, take a loss and spin it into something else. Partly because I agreed to his bid, he bought three more things and I made my margin back on those. That's sometimes how it works. I took a loss on one item but made my money back on something else largely because I was prepared to take that initial loss. Overall, I managed to maintain the 20 per cent I've suggested you work to, which is vital if you're going to progress in the business. Sometimes you're going to make more than 20 per cent. Every now and again you'll double your money, triple it, but you have to learn the basics because it's the basics you always fall back on. I do it. I like doing it. Buying something for £5,000 and selling it for £5,300: a £300 profit. I enjoy the process because it's really quick. Bish-bash-bosh; if you can do that, you will always make a living, even if you take a loss from time to time.

Assuming you haven't taken that loss, come the end of your first month, not only have you got all your buying money back, you've got your profit. What I used to do was split it between money to reinvest in stock and a little bit to keep in reserve. Actually, that's not really true. I used to spend every penny of the profit on stock, bar enough diesel to put in the van and some bread and cream cheese so I could go off and do it all again.

Right from the off I was addicted to the business of finding the best stock I could buy and nothing has changed in the 30 years since. That's the key to success in this business. Just get on with it. Don't moan. Don't complain. Don't be one of those people whinging. This is the business you've chosen to get into. You've worked very hard to be here. Smile every day because,

SELLING

as far as I'm concerned, you're in the best job in the world. The only way to make money is to buy and sell something. You can buy and sell your time if you like, that's fine, but you'll never make any real money. It doesn't matter what it is – commodities, cars, a piece of land, a piece of wood, some slate or a pound of garden seed – to make real money you've got to buy and sell *something*. If you do the right things, acquire the right knowledge and implement the advice I'm offering, you're going to make a lot of money and you're going to have a wonderful time doing it. But you must do two things religiously. Always keep money in your bank and always keep an eye on the money coming in and out on a daily basis. You need to make sure you've got money moving around and that you're always in the black.

4

DOING IT THE RIGHT WAY

In the antiques business, making good decisions about what to buy and selling it well is only part of the story. It's not just what you do, it's how you do it. As I've said many times, your reputation is all important, so the way you conduct yourself is crucial. Remember that you are dealing in luxury goods, not essentials, so people are not obliged to deal with you. But if you act the right way and are true to yourself, you're much more likely to be successful.

Negotiation

The reality is there's no great secret to effective negotiating – in my opinion, openness and honesty are the only real principles you need, especially at the beginning. If you're up against a seasoned dealer (which you probably will be), just be honest. Tell him or her where you are in the trade, that you're just starting out and you don't know a huge amount. Do not try and pull the wool over anyone's eyes, and don't do silly convoluted deals. Show up, look them in the eye, shake their hand firmly and say something like this:

> I'm really interested in this piece that has caught my eye. I'm new to the trade, but I think it's something I could resell. I was wondering what your very best price would be if I buy today, pay you straight away and take it away with me now. I know it's a steep learning curve, so I'd be really grateful for any help you can give me.

Now, if you've been upfront, polite and honest, the chances are the dealer will want to help you. These days the trade isn't like it used to be and most people are stand-up and open. If they think you're being fair with them, then they're likely to be fair with you. They know it's a trade sale and that you need to make a margin. Say they've got a price on it of £700, they'll have paid about £400 and are likely to let you have it for £500. They've made £100 and left you room to make £200 because it's still worth the £700 they're asking – they're giving you your profit. That's the easiest and most consistent form of negotiation. No tricks, no traps, just a straightforward transaction between two people who honour the handshake. If you're going in with a view to doing it any other way – DON'T. It's simple advice but you won't come unstuck if you follow it.

Don't forget, most dealers out there have heard every bullshit line there is. I've had loads, with lads coming in and spinning a story, telling me this, that and the other. But I've heard it all before and won't be fooled – I generally let them witter on and then smile and say, 'No, thank you.' I also won't deal with them ever again. That's the way the trade is: if you get a reputation for 'trying it on', no one will deal with you. If you go to a seasoned dealer and try to take the piss, they will floor you. You'll walk out with nothing, and they'll never want to see you again.

Remember, you're not in the driving seat. This is particularly true when you start out. What you need to do is get the best deal you can without trying to get one over on them. The very best deals are done when everyone appreciates this and everyone walks away happy. I learnt this really early on, starting when I was eight by swapping things. I also remember trying to buy a car worth a few hundred pounds and I only had £50. Somehow I had to talk this guy into selling the car for what I had, and in the end I managed it. They were happy. I was just really honest. I said, 'This is all I've got, but what I can do is clear the driveway for you. I'll pump the tyres up and make sure it's gone tomorrow.' When you've got no choice, when you have to achieve something, that's usually when you do your best negotiating. Most of it is instinct – it comes naturally and can't really be learnt.

The same principles apply when you're the seller. If your prospective buyer is open and honest with you, you're going to be able to deal with them. The worst thing any buyer can do is offer a silly low price on something that's clearly worth the asking price. If they do, it immediately puts your back up. It's disrespectful not just to the person but the trade. As I've said before, make £50 ten times a day (which you can) and you're making a good living.

You Are What You Sell

You are the embodiment of your business – you're its biggest asset. You therefore need to project the right image. The first step is to choose an appropriate name for your business. Names matter, so choose carefully. These days people seem to name their businesses like they're starting a band or some other name that won't stand the test of time. Call yourself something simple, something easy, something catchy that everyone is going to remember. The easiest thing you can do is use your own name. There's nothing wrong with your name – it's who you are and who you are is the reason you've decided to enter this business in the first place.

Next, you have to maintain the right profile. I was in touch with somebody recently who wanted to start up as a dealer. A good kid, he was just as mad keen as you are and asked me to check him out online. I had a look at his website and it was fine. He was working hard, enthusiastic and the whole thing looked OK. Then I looked at his Instagram account and it was lots of pictures of this lad and his mates getting smashed, making stupid faces, rolling around on the grass, stoned, drunk and just dicking about. Now, that's fine if you're a kid, but if it's your business profile, I'm not going to buy anything off you. When you enter this business, you're moving into a different world. You're selling incredible, often unique things and you have to take it seriously. Being a clown when you're trying to sell something is not going to work, so if that's you right now clean up your online act and make sure you look professional.

Get ready to show the world who you are. There are four main social media platforms available at the moment: Facebook, Twitter, Instagram and TikTok. I always think Facebook is there to keep up with your friends and your gran, although Facebook Marketplace seems quite good. Twitter's not really for selling – it's for people who are very good at using words for battering other people they've never met and probably never will. And although TikTok is a growing market, it's not something I have really used. The one presence I think you must have is an Instagram profile. For our business, I've found Instagram to be by far and away the best, so make sure you take advantage of everything it offers.

It's fantastic because it's visual and it's free. You can go on it 24 hours a day and tell everybody in the world what you're selling and it costs you nothing. Genius. It's brilliant. Use it. But also use any other online platform you can in order to get your message across, as long as it leads to tangible sales. That's the key – it doesn't ultimately matter what social media you are on as long as you use it to its best advantage to market yourself and your items.

If you are using multiple platforms simultaneously, make sure you convey the same message across them all, and make sure an item is always the same price across the board. You can't sell something cheaper in one place and more expensively in another. That might seem obvious but I've seen people do it. Keep the message the same and build an online following. The trick then is to make sure you keep it fresh and update it at the same time every day. I usually post between 8 and 8.30pm. Anyone following me will know that's the time to check what's new, and that consistency establishes a connection. If you want to work out the right time for you, your Instagram data should tell you when most people are looking at your profile.

People look at you and what you do and they go: 'I like that. I like you. I like what you are. I like what you're doing.' Because of that they follow you. Other people will look at you and go: 'I don't like that. I don't like you and I don't like what you're doing.' They won't follow you. It's a natural filter. Assuming they're the former, those people will come along for the journey with you and you need to make sure you nurture the relationship. It's a machine that needs to be fed, so you have to keep on doing it. With a following you're able to sell things in new and exciting ways that I barely understood when I sold my first few items online. You collect people in your gang and you feed the gang. You sell them things and you talk to them. You might never meet your online customers, but what you're doing is adding members to your own personal club and that's what works for me.

New stock every day (along with the stories you need to tell) goes a long way to building up an overview of you, your aesthetic, interests and background. You are what you sell. This is all about you. What you're doing is creating the story of not just your business, but your dream, the way you want, and potentially the way they want, to live. You're building a picture around what you're trying to sell. It's a way of putting out there who you are and what you're trying to say. The best dealers have an aesthetic of their own. They'll post pictures of themselves with friends at a party, outside a museum, listening to great music or reading a fantastic book – something that will associate them with an aspect of the business they really love, which is all part of the marketing process. They're projecting a lifestyle around what they're selling, a piece of furniture strategically placed or some wall art or statuary – it doesn't matter. I've posted pictures of my house and shop, maybe my car, and people take a look and identify with what they see. 'That's what I want to be.' Once you've made a connection with people, the next place they go is your website to see if they can buy a bit of the kind of life they've just witnessed – you know what I mean.

The same principles apply when you're dealing with the trade. You establish who you are partly from your online presence, which allows other dealers to build up a reliable and consistent picture of what you represent. That's how trust is established and why projecting the right image on social media is so important. So keep on top of it at all times.

Keeping the Odd Bit

This is a strange subject because the whole point of the antiques trade is to buy and sell very quickly. But then again, the reason you've got into the business in the first place is because you love antiques. I've lost count of the times people have told me their business started out because of the stuff they'd been buying for themselves. When you become a dealer, keeping the odd piece is fine, but it's important to reiterate that when you're first starting out you need to focus solely on turning stock over. That's vital. But let's assume you've been trading a while and you're doing well and something comes across your gunsights and you think: 'I love that. I want it in my house. I want to own that.'

OK, that's fine. You want to keep it (at least for a while). There are two ways of doing it: you can buy it with your own money, or you can buy it with the company's money. But if you use the company's money, remember that you're robbing yourself – because you're tying up funds and not making any profit.

If I were you, I'd buy it with your own money. Put it away. It's yours. There you go – done. You've spent some of your profit and bought that special thing for yourself.

I like to have nice things in my house and there's a reason for that – it's good to live with the items you sell, as you'll understand them and yourself better. But everything an antiques dealer buys will be sold eventually, so remind yourself of that and put a price ticket on it.

Holding on to pieces for long periods of time can be hugely profitable. It can be a very, very clever thing to do; you just want to make sure that all your taxes are paid and all the legal requirements are covered if you use company funds. Now and again I'll buy a specific item to hold for a while through the company because I believe I've got something I think will be worth a lot more money in the future. If I put it away there's every chance I'll realise a far greater profit. On the other hand I might see a particular piece and think it would be really good if I paired it with another. Or I might think it's really good but it's missing a bit and I think I might be able to source what's missing. I might see something that's really good but isn't 'in' right now – but it will be in the future. The more you get into the business, the more knowledge you acquire and the more money you make, the more you can start to do this. You'll come across certain items and understand their future value and be able to make that kind of informed decision.

Every item you buy through the company will be on your books until you come to sell it. That's fine. If you can afford to buy and keep, then do so with items you really, really love and build up a collection. Focus though, and be mindful of selling it eventually – don't get too attached.

You also need to stick to the principles you applied when you first started out in the business. Think about what it is you're collecting. It could be twentieth-century English folk art or Grand Tour bronzes. It might be tramp art or football memorabilia from one particular team. Whatever it is, you build and learn. You study that subject to make sure you buy right and can put together a valuable collection. One day, further down the road, you might have an auction, one big collection of your specialist items, the things you bought to put away. But remember: even when you're buying to keep, everything is a deal. You're ultimately buying to sell no matter how much time there is in between, so keep your business head on when it comes to pricing. Don't let your heart rule to the point you'll never make a profit and don't put so much away that you've got no money. Don't start hoarding. Make sure you're still turning stock over and you can more than afford to hold on to that piece you've bought to sell in the future.

So, you're turning stock over but you can also start to build a collection and that's a very exciting part of the antiques business. When you buy to keep, you're playing the market. It's like trading in stocks and shares: some you buy to keep for a while; some you buy to sell immediately. Be clever with what you're buying and what you're keeping. When the market is right and it's time to sell, do so and start all over again.

I'm always building collections. In the back of my mind there's a future auction with my name on it. I've always got tons of stuff lying around – that's how it is in this business – and eventually it gets to the point you've got so much stuff, you've got no room for it. Or you might need an injection of cash or you're just fed up looking at it. It might be one of the three Ds – Death, Divorce, Debt. Or maybe you want to retire (you'll never retire from this business) so you plan for a distant auction. Lots and lots of dealers do this:

they buy to keep over an entire career then finally, their collection ends up at auction. It's a really good idea, like a little pension fund you build over years and years. You don't have to tell the world – you just buy and put away and wait for the right market. But you mustn't do this to the detriment of your day-to-day business. You have to turn stock over. Money is the tool of your trade and you cannot deal if you don't have any.

I'm in a position now where I buy at least one thing a month (sometimes one a week) that I think will one day feature in a specialist auction. When the right piece comes up and I can afford it, I'll buy something to keep on the books but put it to one side. I'm putting together my own collection of things I think work particularly well together for a single-owner sale. It's not a mish-mash of motoring memorabilia, football memorabilia, Grand Tour, country house, Art Deco, etc. – I'm collating a catalogue of items for a selected auction of the very best of one type of thing for one particular type of buyer. I've been actively doing it for about 15 years and have a huge amount ready. One day I'll have the joy of seeing my name on the auction catalogue. That'll be a day to enjoy, a day when I'm able to realise the fruits of years of labour. But I know what I'm like. When that day finally comes, I'll have a phone line in to another auction, because that's the buzz – that's why I get out of bed.

That buzz never goes away. If you're passionate when you start, the passion never dies. In fact, it gets more intense the longer you are in the business. You're always going to have that so just enjoy it. Enjoy the quick turnaround, the small profit – that's the bread and butter. Then, when you're buying items you might want to hold on to, take them home, display them, live with them, enjoy what you've bought. And have them around you not just for the aesthetic pleasure – if you're constantly looking at them you will always be learning. You can never know enough – read that again – about a particular piece or the period it comes from, the type of craftsman that made it. The more you look the more you learn. When you see another one, when you come across something similar to but better than the one you have, you'll understand the superior piece and why it's more accomplished than the one in your living room. Perhaps it's down to the form, the scale or the detail of the work involved, or maybe it's the colour. Or you might not see a better one – you might come across one that's worse and realise how good your piece is. Remember what we said at the beginning, how you need to look at what's good and bad in your field? Well that's a discipline you always need to stay abreast of. After a while it's instinctive. It comes naturally. The more you know, the better your understanding. There will come a time when you see something and your reaction will be instant. So, have these pieces around you, study them, learn from them. Let the knowledge soak into you.

I love going to antiques dealers' houses because they always keep the best things for themselves; some have incredible taste and extraordinarily good collections. You see their stuff and you're like, 'My god, that's life-changing.' It really can be. The way some of these people put things together is just incredible. The naturally talented dealers are generally also naturally talented interior decorators. You can become that. You can be that good if that's the level you want to get to. There's nothing to stop you. But be true to yourself from the start, otherwise you're going to be playing a part your whole life and that's no good. Be yourself. It's the right way of working.

Things You Shouldn't Say or Do

Seriously, there are things you really shouldn't say in the antiques business. For example, 'My gran had one of those but it was better than that one.' 'I had one of those, but I gave it away.' 'I had one of those and those, and I had that as well.' Those sorts of things are really annoying.

Don't be one of those dealers who asks another dealer all sorts of questions about a particular item with no intention of buying it. If you're looking for knowledge, don't pretend you're interested, and don't try and pull the wool over their eyes – they've been in the trade too long and will see right through you. Just tell them you're learning. Ask if you can pick their brains. Be honest.

Avoid boring conversations about how it used to be. 'Oh, I remember when things were done differently. I remember the old days when we used to ship stuff all round the world. It's not like that any more. There are too many people who don't know what they're doing.' That was then. This is now. Look forward. Don't harp on about the past. Always be looking to what you can be doing. You learn from the past. That's fine. That's good. You're not here to repeat it.

There's nothing more off-putting than playing the 'Big I am'. Don't do it. The best dealers are the ones you never hear about. They're quiet. They tread lightly. They're not shouty. I've been guilty of it in the past and it's embarrassing. Suddenly you've gone from nothing to making a hell of a lot of money and you want to tell everybody. You want the recognition, and it's OK, I suppose, for about five minutes. Get over it and move on – it's boring.

I remember going to a very well-known auction house in Cambridge back in 1999 when I was really beginning to get my stuff together as a dealer. I had some money, a nice car, a warehouse, my first shop. I wandered in thinking, *Happy days. Making money here.* I looked the part, showing up in my Merc estate, wearing a nice jacket and a good-looking pair of brogues. When I viewed the lots, I could see a lot of mid-range smalls – that is, small items such as picture frames and candlesticks, ranging from £300 to £1,500. There were lots of nice things. I thought, *Here we go, I'm going to spend plenty today.*

As I walked in there was a very, very well-known high-end runner there called Harry. Having got what he wanted he was just leaving and hadn't noticed me. Stupidly, and I mean *stupidly*, I spoke to him. I only did it because I wanted him to know I was there. I'm in, one of the gang. I'm a proper dealer and everybody needs to know it. No, they don't. Far better to stay quiet, stay in the background and get on with your job. But not then – then I was full of it, the big man with everything going my way. *Look at me, look at me.* Big mistake, one I was never going to make again.

'Hello, Harry, how are you?'

He stopped in his tracks and looked me right in the eye. 'What're you doing here?'

'What d'you mean? I've come to the auction, same as you.'

He'd been about to leave, remember. He'd already got what he came for but, instead of heading out, he turned round and walked back up to this big fat bloke who was sat right at the front with a woman – they were all but under the rostrum. I made my way to my usual space, back right-hand corner. Harry went up to the fat guy, looked at me then whispered in his ear. The fat guy turned to glance at me, the two of them nodded and Harry left. Having arrived thinking I'd spend 10,000 quid, I sat there all day and didn't get a single item I bid on. The guy in the front made sure I went home completely empty-handed and totally frustrated – he locked me out. He bid me up on everything. Every single thing I went for. I don't know how; he must've had eyes in the back of his head. He must've watched the auctioneer and spotted when he glanced at me and upped his bid accordingly. He completely locked me out. I couldn't understand it.

At the time I could think of nothing I'd done that would make a bloke I'd never seen before completely shut me out of the auction. Pretty quickly I figured it out. The reality of this business is simple. If you haven't got anything to sell you can't make any money. I was the new kid on the block and they saw me as a threat both then and in the future. So, they wanted to send me a message. They wanted rid of me, not just from that auction but completely. The old school was teaching me a lesson. *Don't you come to our auction house thinking you're going to buy this, that and the other. You can't. We will stop you because we can.*

I was there all day and I left with nothing. It cost me an entire day, a load of diesel, a sandwich at lunch and a miserable drive back from Cambridge to North Wales with no stock. Towards the end of the day I worked out what was happening and realised I wasn't going to get anything. But I wasn't going away. Not then. Not ever. I started bidding the other dealer up. Everything he bid on, I did. I did it to annoy him. I did it to let him know I wasn't going to be intimidated. I made sure he paid full price for a load of other stuff I had no interest in.

It was a chastening and irritating experience, but it taught me another really important lesson. Don't be the 'Big I am'. Don't be shouty. Don't use a clarion to let everyone know you're out there. You don't need to. It's always been there in the antiques trade: people like to shout a little, and back then there was always a bit of flash going round. Some dealers liked to tell you how much money they had, what car they were driving, but the truth is, the best business in the antiques trade is done when it's nice and quiet. Keep it simple, straightforward. Don't go shouting about what you're doing. Buy the piece, be quiet about it and get it out the door as quickly as possible. It's not show business. It's the antiques business. Nobody likes a show-off. If you take on board what I'm saying, if you learn from me without making the same mistakes, you'll progress much further and much more quickly than I did.

Similarly, don't brag about how much profit you've made on something. Keep the numbers to yourself. If you sell to the trade, it's really unprofessional to mark it as sold on your website. I always make sure anything a fellow dealer buys from me is deleted from all social media and our website immediately. I expect the same from other dealers and that's how the transactions are treated. It happened with £11,000 worth of chairs I bought the other day. I asked the dealer if he was prepared to delete the items there and then from his website. He said he would. He did it while I watched and we shook hands on the sale. He never owned those chairs. He understands that because they're mine now. When the time is right I need to be able to bring them fresh to the market. That's the primary reason you want a piece deleted. We've all got different customers. The world's a very big place. You'll restore, re-photograph and your customer base will not have seen that piece before so you'll be able to bring it fresh to your marketplace and customers.

When I started it was never done, but I see people doing it now because they want the kudos. They want the world to know they sold that rare piece, that great item, but if you're selling to the trade, you absolutely do not do it. You've sold it. It's gone. It's not yours any more. Have some respect for your fellow dealer whose job it is to sell the piece either further up the trade or via retail. If someone sees the item and asks you if you used to own it, your answer should be: 'I don't know. I don't think so. I had one similar.' This is really important, but some people just don't get it.

People are nosy – there's no one nosier than an antiques dealer. It's our job to be nosy, isn't it? It's our business to know what's going on. But you don't want people finding out what you paid for something. Everything should be on a need-to-know basis. That's not to be secretive for the sake of it, but to give the next dealer in the chain a fair crack at making a profit. Think about it. If you sell something to a dealer and they make money, they'll come back to you. The minute they've sold the thing you sold them, they'll be straight back on your website looking to see what else you've got. They'll want to buy something else they can sell because, as far as they're concerned, you have good items and you're 'lucky'. If you do one good deal, it invariably leads to another. You're making money and they're making money. That's achieved by keeping your head down, working hard and being respectful. If you're in it for the kudos, if you're in it to be the 'Big I am', you'll make some money for a period of time but you will not make it long term. My advice would be to forget things like kudos altogether. Don't be that person. The only way you learn is by listening. These are all lessons I've learnt the hard way. I've made the mistake of thinking I was important, that I'd arrived. As I said, I've tried to be the 'Big I am' (I never was or want to be) and it did nothing except make me look foolish. Don't do that. There's no need for you to make the mistakes I did.

Respect and discretion are all important – treat a dealer the right way and they'll always want to deal with you. These days the first thing anyone seems to say when they come into the shop is: 'What's your best price?' They only do that because it's what they've seen on all those rubbish television programmes. Either that or they look at the price on the label and offer you something ludicrous which you're never going to accept in a month of Sundays. It happens all the time and it does my head in. Making stupid bids does nothing but denigrate the business. If you're going to try and knock someone down, don't be an arsehole about it. What's something worth? What can you get for it? How much are you prepared to pay? If you know you're not even going to be in the same ballpark then don't waste someone's time with a ridiculous bid. Walk away.

It all comes down to respect. You should have respect for the person from whom you've bought an item, and they should have respect for you. And you should have respect for the person you sell it to.

Keep Going

Perseverance is the only way to succeed. If you're not in it you can't win it, but be prepared for a rollercoaster ride. The ups and downs can be incredible. One day you're absolutely smashing it, doing thousands of pounds, then the next day there's nothing. And the day after that and the one after that and the one after that. That's how it can go but there are things you can do.

Equally, there are times when you've had a really good run and you haven't got the stock to replace what you've sold. Supply has dried up and you can't afford that so you just have to keep going. That's what I mean about working 24-7. There is no antiques supplier to phone up and place an order for stock then go to bed and forget about it till it's delivered. That situation doesn't exist. You have to do what you've always done, which is to go out and find it. Get in your car. Talk to other dealers. Go to auctions. Turn up at the fairs. If nothing's shifting on your website or Instagram, load up the car and drive it around to all the dealers you know – do whatever it takes to keep the ball rolling. Turn money over. If you have to cut your margin, do it. If you have to 'push' an item, do it. Keep going. Keep moving. Do not stand still. You won't survive if you do. The trick is always to keep money flowing. But keep a little bit in reserve as well – you need that back-up, remember? That's really hard because the temptation to buy absolutely loads of stock and spend every single penny can be all-consuming. It never goes away. I'm not going to lie; you have to keep tabs on it.

If things grind to a shuddering halt, then create something. If you haven't got much money, go halves with a friend on something. Get something that needs restoration and sell it as it is or sell it in parts. If you're sitting on stock that's not shifting, put some into an auction. Swap something and try and sell that instead. Sell something on commission for somebody – do anything to keep the money rolling. There's always a way of making money in this business.

That's how I started and there's only been one time when I really didn't have any money. I mean none. Not even enough to put diesel in the car or food in my stomach. I literally couldn't feed myself. It was 28 years ago, but I still remember; I got home and had no money because I'd spent it all on stock. I mean all of it, my last penny. I went to look for some food and there was none.

'Bugger, what am I going to do?'

There was nothing I could do, and I went to bed hungry. But I only had to do it once. It was enough to wake me up and teach me not to spend all my money. And I turned things around by going out and selling some of my stock. You just have to keep going.

Even when things are going really well and you're making plenty of money, you've got great stock and really good clients, you're racing and you know what you're doing for the next month, two, maybe three, don't take your foot off the pedal. I never stop buying the right things. If I've got loads and loads of money,

I'll carry on buying but I'll make sure I'm buying right and I'm not blowing all my money. If you've got a ton of cash in the bank don't just go and waste it – wait. Do your due diligence. Use your discretion. Never buy anything that you're not feeling really good about. Don't do it. It's incredibly hard to not buy – one of the hardest things to do is say no – because you always see a profit in things after a bit of work, but you need to keep your enthusiasm in check. Always keep in mind that the next thing you buy should be as good as, if not better than, the last piece you sold. Do that and you won't go wrong. Do it with your private collection and do it with your stock. It keeps the standard up. You should always be trying to improve the quality of what you're selling.

Just as important is making sure your customer service is as good as it can be. The same with your photography and listings. You should never stop trying to improve your restorations. You should strive to ensure that the parts you source for a piece are as authentic as possible. You continually need to make everything about your presence in the antiques trade better, even if you've got a million pounds in the bank, a million pounds' worth of stock, a fabulous shop. If you've got every angle boxed off, keep working hard, and do not rest on your laurels.

There is no let-up to the antiques business. There's no end to it. My mate Tee, who does the TV programme with me, reckons there'd be a really good business in building old people's homes for antiques dealers so you could have a load of dealers in a room and fill it full of stuff they can sell between them, like a constant game of Monopoly – there'd be no need for the telly. Not that antiques dealers ever retire. A few do, I suppose, but most of us go on till we drop, in some form or another – it's a job for life. That's the joy of the business. Antiques dealing is something you get better at. The more you learn the more you know. The more you know the more discerning you become. The more discerning you become the better you're going to be at spotting real quality. The better the quality, the better your inventory, client base and so on. The trick is to stay in the game. Keep going.

What we've discussed goes a long way to establishing the kind of dealer you want to be and it's important to stress again that there is no specific endgame: you can go as far as you want with it and not go any further. No one's going to judge you, least of all me. It's a business where you naturally find the level you want to work at. If you want to be a runner, it doesn't mean you're going to be any less respected by other dealers – in most cases, you are more respected – and it doesn't mean you're not as good as them or you're not going to make more money. Wherever you decide to pitch your business, just make sure you're the best at it. If you want to be the person who sells at antiques fairs out of the back of a van, be the best at it. If you want to be a runner, be the best runner out there. If you want a high street shop, make sure yours is the best shop. But regardless of what level you want to be at, you need to be constantly learning, constantly thinking, constantly on it. The best dealers are multitaskers, utterly focused. They can be a bit ruthless, and they're extremely clever with a fabulous eye.

I said at the beginning that this is a journey, one you'll probably be on for the rest of your life, and there is no destination. It goes on and on and you need clientele to pay for it. That can be other dealers, the public or a mixture of both – it doesn't matter – but you cannot make the journey without them. As far as the world is concerned, anybody can be an antiques dealer, but buying something then trying to sell it does not make you one – far from it. The first few deals you do only indicate the fact you're starting out on that journey. It's a lifetime's work, an incredible adventure, one that can lead anywhere if you're prepared to put in the time as well as the effort you need to acquire the knowledge, the education we talked about. Just because you got a part-time job and have saved enough money for your first tranche of stock doesn't make you the 'rock star' of the trade, although some who come into the business think that's what they're going to be. You *could* be the next big thing – you never know. In 30 years, I've only come across two or three dealers who totally blew me away. They're the ones with a pure aesthetic, something artistic and visual. They knew what they wanted. They knew what they were about. They knew what they liked and they were able to relate that to people like me with the pieces they bought just like a rock star does with music or an artist with paint. The ability to do that, the foresight and vision, has always blown me away and still does.

So, let's recap. You're through the first month or quarter, and you've got some money in your pocket. You can afford to put fuel in your car, so you go and do what you've just done again. Then you do it again. And again. You keep doing it, the same things, the things that have worked so far. You apply the same principles over and over. You do your homework, you research, you learn, building up an inventory of knowledge until what you're doing is second nature. You eat, sleep and breathe the antiques business.

Your next month might be your best one ever, but the month after that might be your worst one. There are certain months of the year that aren't great. August and September, for example, when a lot of the interior designers go on holiday. So do the French, and that's a big market. Halfway through December everything seems to die, and in January everyone's paying their tax. So, that gives you eight or nine months – make sure you coin it in.

It's like being at sea – there are highs and lows, and the highs are really high and the lows incredibly low. The trick is to keep doing it. I cannot stress this enough. I heard a wonderful saying from America: 'Keep turning up'. If want to get fit and cycle up the hill, keep turning up. Keep doing it and eventually you'll get good at it. Nothing worth having is easy. Nothing worth having isn't hard won. That's never been truer than in this era of instant but hollow gratification, and it's very true of the antiques business.

Some people have more of a natural aptitude than others. Some are instantly brilliant. I wasn't. I was good at seeing a deal, and I was good at extracting the profit from something, but I wasn't instantly brilliant. I've been doing this as a job since I was 16 years old and I'm now in my fifties. Despite the years of experience, I don't think I know any more than 1 per cent of what there is to know about the business. There are a thousand different ways to make money and you've got to pick what works for you and know all of the other options.

In terms of setting goals and targets, it's different from most other businesses. There's only one real maxim: keep going. If it ain't broke, don't fix it. Don't start looking a year, two years in advance. Don't give yourself unreasonable expectations. Spend the first five to ten years getting your grounding. This is your apprenticeship. Put in the miles, the time, the reading. The best dealers I know did exactly what we're talking about. They bought and sold lots and lots of things when they first got going. That's how they learnt. If you don't know anything about something when you buy it, you'll know a hell of a lot more when you sell it. You learn really quick when you buy something. This is really important. When you buy an item, you might know a little bit about it and think, I really fancy that, I'll have a go at it. Then you do your homework. Then you set about finding out everything there is to know about that item. Now, when you come to sell it, you're credible, and you're knowledgeable.

It's also important not to compare yourself with anyone else – all that will do is depress you. You're starting from scratch and from a different place to anyone else, so you can't make comparisons. You might know absolutely nothing and someone else might be coming from a fine art background. It doesn't matter. It doesn't necessarily make them better than you. I know a guy who spent 20 years working for another dealer: 20 years clearing up, making tea, arranging foreign travel, fairs, shops, delivery, restoration. He went out on his own, and, on the face of it, he had absolutely everything going for him. He should've hit the ground running and been the best dealer, but he wasn't. He was terrible. He had no independent work ethic. His attitude was all wrong – grumpy, negative – and his buying was all over the place. He should've been brilliant but he wasn't. So make no comparisons. This is your journey, no one else's.

I don't know everything – no one does. Experts are there to be proved wrong. The most important thing is that you find your own place in this world. You will. I promise you. If you don't, if it's not happening, work harder, change it. If it's what you really want, you will get there.

You're at the start of a life-changing journey. It's going to be a hell of a ride, so enjoy it. It's worth the risk.

ACKNOWLEDGEMENTS

Special thanks to Ruth Ellis, Matt Nicholls, Jeff Gulvin, Mohammed Asif, Gordon Stewart, Charlotte, Grace, Tom, Gabriel, Clementine and my mum.